To Liam, Theron, Soren, and Jane

# Contents

# The Programs

# Preface

The bicycle is a vehicle that can clear your mind, improve your health, and make your day more enjoyable. We, the authors, have benefited positively from cycling, and we are addicted to the sport. On a bike we have raced the world, toured the countryside, ridden off road in the mountains, and picked up our milk on the way home from work. Cycling will forever be a part of our lives because it has improved our daily quality of life. We hope this book will help you add the pleasure of cycling to your life.

Cycling is a growing sport in the United States, and the popularity of Lance Armstrong has raised cycling enthusiasm throughout the world. Riders like Lance are excellent role models for cyclists of all levels; however, in addition to inspiration, riders who want to do more than merely "go on a ride" need specific instruction in how to gain fitness as a cyclist and build a training program. The workouts in this book aim to assist the athlete who has on average one hour a day to work out.

Whether you are a beginner or have previous cycling experience, whether you are old or young, or whether you intend to cycle in the mountains, on the flats, or indoors on an ergometer, this book shows you how to succeed. It provides the basics of getting started in the sport of cycling: purchasing your first bike and other cycling gear, mastering your position, assessing your fitness, getting started on a training program, peaking for a race, and keeping injury free and motivated.

The book is split into three parts. Part I begins by helping you with the sometimes overwhelming process of equipment selection. We evaluate numerous options in bicycles, gear, and clothing to help you make the best choices. You will learn step-by-step the process of developing the proper position on the bike so that you are comfortable, which will help make your riding experience enjoyable instead of a chore. We teach you how to pedal efficiently and use your gears to optimize your strength.

We help you refine your bike-handling skills and provide advice on where to ride, making your cycling safer.

Part I also offers instruction on the basics of cycling physiology and how to assess your cycling fitness. Training guidelines will help you start your program. You'll learn how to find your maximum heart rate and your lactate threshold, which you will use to individualize your training program. In part I, you will also learn how to prevent and treat common cycling injuries through proper stretching and other techniques.

Once you're set up and are confident pedaling your bicycle, you will be ready to benefit physically. Part II includes 60 workouts that will take you from your first few rides to longer, more intense efforts. The workouts are simple to follow and are organized based on five different intensities: building an endurance base, improving lactate threshold, climbing, time-trialing, and sprinting. These workouts offer plenty of variety to help you remain stimulated and motivated.

Part III shows you how to develop a training program by plugging these workouts into a periodized plan. We have outlined the training programs that we have used to gain physiological benefits. Included are three sample programs for the beginner, intermediate, and advanced cyclist. We used programs similar in structure while training for races such as the World Championships and the Olympics. The goal of part III is to help you improve your fitness and health through an individualized cycling training program.

Cycling can be enjoyed at all ages and all levels. The commuter, bike tourist, century rider, avid racer, and weekend warrior can all benefit both psychologically and physically from riding a bike. There is nothing like the feeling you get when you arrive home after a great ride and put your legs up. You'll see.

# Acknowledgments

We are very excited to have worked on this project. We treasured the experience of getting to work with friends, the result of which has brought us even closer together. We would not be where we are today if it weren't for our friends, families, mentors, coaches, and teammates.

We are thankful to Connie and Davis Phinney, who presented us with this project. They have been longtime mentors as well as excellent friends and role models. Davis was diagnosed with Parkinson's disease in 2001 and recently started the Davis Phinney Foundation (DPF) to raise money for Parkinson's research. Davis and Connie's commitment to the DPF and their family is inspiring.

Our parents have been exceptional and provided us all with a nurturing environment. They supported us in all our endeavors—teaching us discipline, compassion, and the importance of family. Thanks to all of you: Francis and Margadette Demet, Michael John and Clare Barry, and Karl and Linda Smith.

While in college, Shannon became great friends with a fellow cyclist named Allen Lim. Shannon and Allen raced together, trained together, and began to develop a passion for exercise physiology. Allen would later embark upon graduate studies in physiology, while Shannon pursued an education in medicine. They always planned to combine their two careers some day, and that plan is now a reality with the launch of Thrive Health and Fitness Medicine (Thrive HFM). As if it were meant to be, Allen then became friends with Dede and Michael while studying in Boulder, Colorado. Through this common connection, Dede, Michael, and Shannon also became great friends. So, in a way, we owe the creation of this book to Dr. Allen Lim. Thanks, Allen, for stimulating our minds, striving for excellence, and being such a good friend.

**Dede and Michael**—We would like to thank USA Cycling, the Canadian Cycling Association, and all the coaches and physiologists who have had a profound impact on our understanding of cycling, training, and exercise physiology.

**Shannon**—I would like to thank all those individuals who helped shape my life experience and all the faculty and physicians who have educated me along the way. Thanks to Dr. "Maha" Mahadevan for being an inspiration and teaching me how to be a good doctor. Thanks to Peter Thomsen for being my role model. Thanks to my sister, Melissa, and her husband, Ben, for their friendship. Finally, thanks to my wife, Jane, who not only keeps me grounded and pointed in the right direction, but also is my best friend.

# The Essentials

Cycling is a fantastic sport. It provides an excellent cardiovascular workout, and cyclists of all ages and levels can enjoy it. In part I, you will first learn how to make your initial purchases and then move on to learning the fundamentals of proper training.

Chapter 1 provides the information you need to make the right choice when purchasing a bike, cycling gear, and clothing. This chapter introduces the different types of bikes, their specifications, and their various uses. It also describes the various gear and clothing that can improve your performance and make your cycling more comfortable.

Once you're set to go, chapter 2 focuses on positioning. You will learn guidelines for setting up your bike to provide the optimal position for comfort and performance. You will also learn the fundamentals of pedaling dynamics, efficiency, gearing, and shifting, which will help you move quickly and comfortably on your bicycle. This chapter highlights the importance of obeying cycling laws, taking safety precautions, and improving bike-handling skills. This information will help better your performance and your cycling safety. Finally, chapter 2 offers advice on choosing the best roads and trails for your training.

In chapter 3, you will learn how to train effectively through guidelines based on adaptation, workload variables, and periodization. You learn to assess your goals, individualize your training plan, and track your cycling progress.

Once you have started riding and are comfortable on your bike, you will learn how to assess your fitness level through an understanding of basic exercise physiology, and you will learn how to determine your maximum heart rate and lactate threshold through fitness testing. With the information provided in chapter 4, you will be able to determine your fitness level and develop a training plan that suits your needs.

Chapter 5 shows you how to take care of yourself by warming up, cooling down, and developing a stretching routine. Chapter 5 also addresses common cycling injuries, such as saddle sores, road rash, and overuse injuries and provides instruction on how to best care for them—and, better yet, how to avoid them.

The information in these chapters provides you with the fundamentals to get started in the sport and gives you a head start in your cycling training. It may sound complicated at the outset, but with the plan we have set out, the puzzle will come together with ease, and you'll soon be out enjoying a ride while improving your overall health.

# CHAPTER 1

# Choosing Cycling Equipment

The first step in a training program is finding and purchasing the proper equipment. It is important to invest in gear that will provide comfort, safety, and performance. Your equipment requirements will vary according to your fitness and training goals. Your choices are almost limitless and can seem overwhelming, but armed with basic knowledge, you will be able to choose equipment that will meet your needs. This chapter will help you make informed choices when purchasing gear.

## Types of Bicycles

If you do not already own a bike or if you are in the market for a new one, you must assess your goals as a cyclist before purchasing a bike. There are many different types of bicycles for different types of riding; therefore, you must match your bike with the primary type of riding you will do. For example, if you will always ride on paved surfaces, you want a road bike with narrow, smooth tires that decrease drag and ground friction as well as a light frame that will decrease weight and make going up hills easier. On the flip side, if riding off road is your passion, then you should purchase a mountain bike with a sturdier frame than a road bike and with bigger, knobby tires that grab the dirt for traction.

If you like to tour through the countryside and plan to haul changes of clothing, tents, or other items, you may want a touring bike with fittings for racks that carry bags. If you're unsure about the type of riding you'll do, there are bikes that fall between these categories. A sport recreation bike is a versatile choice. It is light enough for recreational racing but is also set up with fittings to carry racks and fenders for road-touring trips. If you are an avid road racer or triathlete, a specialized racing bicycle is the ideal choice. If you will compete in time trials or triathlons, you may also want to purchase a second, time trial-specific bicycle.

Hybrids and cyclocross bikes allow you to ride comfortably on both road and dirt trails. A cyclocross bike is used for riding and racing of a more competitive nature. Perhaps you've seen pictures of muddy riders running with bikes slung over their shoulders. They are most likely participating in a cyclocross event. Hybrid bikes have larger tires for increased stability and offer the recreational rider a more comfortable and upright position than do road and mountain bikes. They are ideal for simple dirt roads and city riding. They are easy to maneuver in traffic and comfortable to ride while wearing casual clothing.

## Road Bikes

Road bicycles are light, aerodynamic, and built for riding at high speeds on pavement. They are specially designed for riders who want to ride faster, longer, and undertake an aerobically intense workout; however, you can get a good workout on any type of bicycle. In general, road bikes have smooth, narrow tires, standard turned-down handlebars, multiple gears, and skinny saddles (see figure 1.1). Tire sizes are denoted as the diameter of the wheel (from the hub to the outside of the tire along the radial of the spoke) and by the width of the tire at its widest point (i.e., 27 inches × 1.25 inches). Common diameters for road bike tires are 26 inches (650c) and 27 inches (700c). Note that the c (as in "700c") originated as a notation on French tires and does not stand for an exact unit of measurement. Tire width ranges from 18 to 32 millimeters, or 1 to 1.25 inches.

The way in which the sizing of bike tires, rims, wheels, and tubes has changed over the years and can be very confusing. Subtle differences can be huge when assembling equipment for your saddle bag, which contains your equipment for fixing flat tires. To ensure your rolling accessories are compatible, consult with your local bike shop when buying replacement parts.

Road bikes also offer a range of gearing. Depending on whether your bike has a double or triple chainring in the front—that is, has two or three chainrings connected to the crank—the bike will have 14 to 30

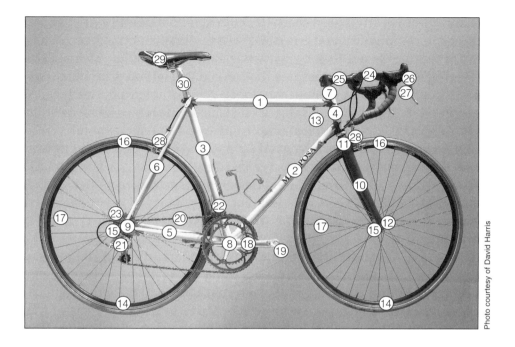

**Frame:**
1　Top tube
2　Down tube
3　Seat tube
4　Head tube
5　Chain stays
6　Seat stays
7　Head set (steering bearings)
8　Bottom bracket (crank bearings)
9　Rear drop-outs

**Fork:**
10　Fork blades
11　Fork crown
12　Front drop-outs
13　Steering column (inside head tube)

**Wheels:**
14　Rims
15　Hubs with quick release
16　Tires and inner tubes
17　Spokes and nipples

**Transmission:**
18　Crankset (cranks and chainrings)
19　Pedals
20　Chain
21　Rear derailleur
22　Front derailleur
23　Sprocket (cassette)

**Handlebars, brakes, and saddle:**
24　Handlebar
25　Stem
26　Brake levers
27　Gear shifters
28　Brakes
29　Saddle
30　Seat post

**Figure 1.1** Major parts of a road bike.

gears. Although this may seem like an excessive amount of gearing, the extra options will come in handy when pedaling up a steep climb or trying to pass another cyclist while riding downhill at high speed. Road bikes have skinny saddles that are lightweight and, while it may seem contrary to common sense, more comfortable than their wider counterparts during longer rides. If you plan to ride for less than an hour at a time, a cushioned, wider saddle may be more comfortable.

Frame technology has advanced a great deal in the past 10 years. Not only is designing a frame an art, it is also a science. Today's frame builders apply the same techniques in designing new frames and choosing materials that Boeing uses in designing its airplanes. If you took chemistry in high school, you can put the information you learned to good use when you walk into a bike shop—a tangible display of the periodic table of the elements. Frames can be made of carbon fiber, aluminum, magnesium, titanium, steel, or a combination of these. Frames have become so light that some manufacturers have had to add weight to frames used in the Tour de France in order to meet the criteria of the Union Cycliste Internationale (UCI, or International Cycling Union). The lightest frames on the market are carbon or aluminum. Titanium and light steel frames are slightly heavier than aluminum and carbon models, but they are generally more durable and give the most comfortable ride. The difference in weight is negligible to all but the most serious cyclists, but the difference in expense can be significant. A good rule of thumb when purchasing cycling equipment based on weight is: If the cost is more than a dollar per gram in savings, it is not worth the extra expense. Base models start at $600.

## Touring Bikes

Touring bikes generally have heavier frame tubing and a more relaxed geometry (i.e., more shallow head tube angle and seat tube angle) than road bikes. Touring bikes also have eyelets at various locations to which you attach racks and fenders so that you can carry your luggage in bags while riding. Similar to road bikes, touring bikes come with a range of gears—usually 24 to 30 different gears—for riding on all types of terrain and carrying extra luggage. Because of the heavier tubing, extra gears, and racks, touring bikes generally weigh more than road bikes. Touring bikes usually have 27-inch (700c) wheels like a road bike, but are normally fitted with fatter tires, 28 to 35 millimeters (1.1-1.4 inches). The increased tire width makes the bikes more suitable for rougher surfaces and for carrying heavier loads. The relaxed geometry and wider tires increase road-shock absorbency and ride comfort. Michael Barry's father spent his career designing and building specialized touring bikes, and the options available are impressive. Base models start at $750.

## Sport Recreation Bikes

Sport recreation bikes are versatile and therefore are a good choice for beginning cyclists. They bridge the gap between a racing bike and a true touring bike. They accommodate riders who do mostly day rides but on occasion want to venture into longer tours or recreational racing. These bikes generally offer a wider range of gears than a racing bike and have fittings for racks to accommodate the possibility of touring. They can also be competitive in entry-level racing because they are generally lighter than a touring bike. Sport recreation bikes offer more comfort than road bikes because the rider sits in a more upright position and the wider tires provide shock absorbency. Like touring and road bikes, sport recreation bikes are usually equipped with 27-inch (700c) wheels and the tires are usually 23 to 28 millimeters (0.9-1.1 inches). Base models start at around $700.

Photo courtesy of Michael Barry Sr.

**Figure 1.2**  A sport recreation bike.

## Mountain Bikes

If riding over rough terrain and coming home muddy appeals to you, then you definitely want to look into purchasing a mountain bike. Mountain bicycles are specially designed for cyclists who want to ride off road. They have rugged, strong components and frames intended for rough, abusive treatment. The fat, knobby tires offer more traction and cushioning than do the tires of the other types of bikes, and flatter-profile handlebars place the rider in a more upright seated position (see figure

**Figure 1.3** A mountain bike.

1.3). This position shifts the rider's weight to the back tire, giving the rider more traction when riding in loose dirt. Unlike road tires, which are measured in both the English and metric system, mountain bike tires are primarily measured in inches. The reason is most likely because mountain biking has its roots in the United States. Wheel diameters are usually 26 inches, and the width can range from 1.95 to 2.2 inches. Because these bikes are often ridden up steep mountain terrain, they generally have a triple chainring in the front with 21 to 27 gears. Most higher-end models have suspension systems built into the fork or the rear triangle (or both) for shock absorption. Although mountain bikes can be used on the road, they have a slower rolling speed because of their smaller wheel size, increased wind resistance, and heavier weight. Prices usually start at $400.

## Hybrid and Cyclocross Bikes

One of our favorite rides outside of Boulder, Colorado, is the "cross-bike loop." This ride takes us up into the mountains over varying terrain. It starts on pavement, moves to a dirt jeep road, hits a section of mountain bike trail, and then spits us back out onto the pavement. A cyclocross bike is the preferred machine to handle this variation in terrain. Both hybrid and cyclocross bicycles can handle diverse terrain by offering more agility and speed than wide-tire, 26-inch-wheel mountain bikes and are still adequately equipped to handle off-road riding. Hybrid bicycles best suit recreational cyclists who ride primarily on pavement with an occasional excursion onto a dirt road. They also are a good option for someone who feels unstable on a road bike but does not want to buy a mountain bike. Cyclocross bikes are a bit more hard-core and are intended primarily for racing cyclocross on courses containing road and off-road sections with obstacles that competitors must clear by dismounting and carrying the bike. However, these bikes have recently become more popular as all-around bikes. Many people are discovering the joys of riding over all kinds of terrain just as we have found in the mountains surrounding Boulder.

Most hybrid and cyclocross bikes have 27-inch (700c) wheels and 21 to 30 gears. Models with 26-inch (600c) wheels are also available. These bikes are sometimes equipped with shock-absorbing seat posts and handlebar stems. Hybrids usually have either straight-across handlebars (see figure 1.4) that cause the rider to lean forward slightly or cruiser bars that curve back toward the rider, who sits more upright. Cyclocross bikes have turned-down (or "drop") handlebars like on a road bike. Cyclocross bikes are usually lighter than hybrid bicycles. Prices for hybrids start at around $400, and cyclocross bikes start at around $700.

**Figure 1.4** A hybrid bike.

Photo courtesy of Trek Bicycles (www.trekbikes.com)

## Time Trial Bikes

Time trial bikes are road bikes aerodynamically designed and specially fitted for racing in timed road events and triathlons. Time trial bikes are designed for maximal speed, not maximal comfort. They place the rider in an extremely aerodynamic tucked position that is not particularly comfortable for long distances; therefore, they don't make good everyday bikes. Racers who own time trial bikes consider them a secondary bike and use them for specialized training and racing only. Time trial bikes have 14 to 20 gears and usually have 27-inch (68.6 cm) wheels. They have smooth, narrow, streamlined tires and rims (19-23 mm [0.75-0.90 in]) and special aerodynamic handlebars with gear shifters built into the tips. These handlebars allow riders to position their arms on armrests out in front of the body. This lowers the head and chest and helps break the wind over the rest of the body. The low, stretched out position is not comfortable for long rides, but it serves the purpose of riding fast well. The aerodynamic position and components reduce frontal surface area, and as a result, reduce drag. Unless you plan to race against the clock, put the purchase of this bike on hold. Prices start at around $1,000.

# Cycling Gear

Having the right gear can make your cycling experience safer and more comfortable. However, choosing among the different types and brands can be overwhelming to experienced and less-experienced cyclists alike. The information in the following sections will help you select the best options for your unique needs and prioritize your purchases based on your budget. Table 1.1 on page 11 provides a list of items and price ranges for various levels of cycling.

## Tires

We recommend equipping your bike with clincher tires rather than sew-ups or tubular tires. Tubular tires are specialized racing tires that professionals use. They are lightweight and made of special, low resistance compounds. But, with decreased weight comes decreased durability. Tubulars are also more expensive than clinchers and must be glued onto the rim by a skilled mechanic. We can tell you from experience, it is no fun to be screaming around a corner in a race and have your tubular roll off your rim because the glue broke down or was placed incorrectly. Clincher tires are less expensive than tubular tires and contain an inner tube that the rider can easily replace when

## Table 1.1 Equipment Costs

### Basic Equipment

| | | |
|---|---|---|
| Helmet | | $40+ |
| Cycling shoes | Touring | $45-125 |
| | Racing | $60-400 |
| | Off-road (mountain shoes) | $50-200 |
| Saddlebag | | $15 |
| Spare tubes | | $5 |
| Tire irons | | $5 |
| Tire-patch kit | | $5 |
| Portable bike pump | | $25 |
| Air cartridges | | $10 |
| Multitool | | $20 |
| Water bottle | | $5 |
| Water bottle cage | | $15-30 |
| Cycling clothing | Cycling shorts | $35-125 |

### Intermediate Equipment

| | | |
|---|---|---|
| Bike computer | | $30-60 |
| Heart rate monitor | | $75-400 |
| Eyewear | | $60+ |
| Cycling clothing | Jerseys | $35-85 |
| | Gloves | $20-35 |
| | Jacket | $75+ |
| | Tights | $40-80 |
| | Arm and leg warmers | $20-50 |

### Advanced Equipment

| | | |
|---|---|---|
| Power meter | | $700-3,000 |

the inevitable flat tire occurs. Many different models of clinchers are available, and your choice will depend on the type of riding you plan to do. For training, you may want wide and thick treads for better traction and prevention of flats. For racing, you may switch to smoother, light and narrow treads for increased speed and aerodynamics. Inner tubes vary in material, weight, and puncturability. Discuss your needs with a salesperson at your local bike shop if you aren't sure which type of clincher tires and tubes to purchase. A set of clincher tires with tubes will cost you $65 to $125.

Mountain bikes are unique because you can equip them with either clincher tires or tubeless tires. Higher-end mountain bikes now use technology similar to that used in car tires. As the name implies, a tubeless mountain bike tire eliminates the need for a tube (and in theory, reduces the possibility of a flat tire on the trail). The tire creates a direct seal between the rim and tire. To prevent small leaks, the tire contains a foam sealant that will obstruct a small puncture. However, if a large puncture occurs, you must replace and refit the tire. We recommend tubeless tires for mountain bikes because they allow you to run the tire at low pressures, which improves traction, and they decrease the frequency of pinch flats that occur with clincher-type tires. If cost is an issue, clinchers do a fine job and don't leave you wondering where your money went.

## Helmets

A bicycle helmet reduces the risk of serious head injury. It is risky to ride without one, and spending money for a high-quality bicycle helmet is an investment in your life and future. A good helmet will last for years, as long as it is not abused or involved in a crash. If you crash and hit your helmet, replace it. Bicycle shops carry the best selection at different prices, but you should expect to pay at least $40. You may also find helmets in sporting good, toy, department, and discount stores.

Since April 1999, the Consumer Product Safety Commission (CPSC) inspects all bike helmets. You can consider safe any helmet designed for cycling that carries a sticker stating that it meets the standards of the Canadian Standards Association (CSA), the British Standards Institution (BSI), American Standards Institute (ASI), Snell, or the American Society for Testing and Materials (ASTM).

You must also make sure your helmet fits properly so it will be in place if an impact occurs. To choose the right size, try on several different helmets before buying one. Take the time to try different pad and strap positions. In a bike shop, a salesperson can help you find the proper fit. Helmets come in many different colors, styles, and designs, so you should be able to find a helmet that you like. It is easier to wear a helmet if you get one that is comfortable and looks good.

## Pedals and Shoes

Cycling pedals and shoes are important because they connect you to your bike. Both good handling and efficient transfer of power from your body to the bicycle require a strong link between your foot and the pedal. The shoes and cleats you select will depend on the type of riding you plan to do and on the type of pedals you choose for your bike.

In the past, the only method for securing a cyclist's feet to the pedals was with toe clips and straps. Some riders still prefer this method, but it's considered retro. Today, the majority of cyclists use clipless pedal systems. Clipless pedals start at $65.

Clipless pedal systems eliminate the use of clips and straps by holding your foot to the pedal with a cleat-and-binding system. In these systems, the shoe locks into the pedal and is released by the rider twisting his or her ankle sideways in a method similar to that used with ski bindings. Some clipless pedals keep your foot in a fixed position. Other clipless pedals allow a degree of movement, or *float*; these are recommended to prevent knee injuries. Whichever type of pedal you decide to use, your cleats must correspond to it (purchased pedals routinely include the appropriately matched cleats). Cycling cleats can be removed from the shoe and adjusted to ensure a proper fit with your bike and cycling position. While numerous cleat-and-pedal systems exist, they all fall into two categories: (1) racing cleats and pedals, and (2) touring and off-road cleats and pedals.

Racing cleats are mounted into the soles of racing shoes. Racing-shoe soles are extremely stiff and often made of carbon fiber, titanium, or plastic; their rigidity helps to efficiently transfer energy from the cyclist's leg to the pedals. While racing shoes and cleats are efficient for riding, the cleats are bulky and rigid and make walking difficult and uncomfortable. This generally is not a problem in road cycling because your feet have limited contact with the ground. However, if you do plan to frequently dismount your bike during rides, there are models of racing shoes available to make walking and running easier. Cyclists who intend to compete in road races or use the bike primarily for training should choose a racing shoe along with a racing pedal-and-cleat-system. Expect to pay $60 to $400 for a pair of racing shoes.

Touring and off-road cleat-and-pedal systems have a smaller cleat recessed into a sole that is more flexible than that of a racing shoe. These cleat systems are often referred to generically as SPD (after *Shimano Pedaling Dynamics*, one of the original and most successful recessed cleat systems). Because of the recessed cleat, touring and off-road shoes are more comfortable to walk in than racing shoes. If you plan to tour or ride off road, or if you plan to do a lot of stopping and sightseeing while cycling, choose a touring or off-road pedal system and shoe.

Touring shoes look similar to running shoes but have stiffer and integrated cleats that bind to the pedal. Expect to pay $45 to $125 for touring shoes.

Off-road shoes (also called *mountain shoes*) look similar to low-top hiking shoes. The soles of these shoes are more rugged and flexible than a road shoe. The added flexibility of these shoes is necessary because off-road cyclists come in contact with the ground fairly often. A trail might require the cyclist to dismount and hike or run with the bike to clear obstacles. Off-road shoes are available for both standard and clipless pedal systems, and some styles can be used with either system. Expect to pay $50 to $200 for off-road shoes.

Cycling shoes are an important purchase. If you find yourself overwhelmed by the number of options, find a knowledgeable salesperson to advise and fit you in the proper shoe based on the type of riding you will be doing.

## Saddlebags, Tools, and Bike Pumps

Flat tires are inevitable while cycling; therefore, it is best to learn how to change your own tires so that you are not left stranded. If you have never fixed a flat, ask a repairman at a bike shop or a friend to show you how. Stay prepared with a properly equipped saddlebag ($15) that attaches to the seat post under your bike seat. In your saddlebag you need two spare bike tubes ($5+), two tire irons ($5+), and a patch kit ($5). You also need a portable bike pump ($25+) that can be mounted on your bike, or air cartridges ($10) that fit into your saddlebag. It is a good idea to carry a multitool ($20) in your saddlebag, which can be used to fix most mechanical problems that occur out on the road. The multitool has allen keys in several different sizes and screwdrivers and often includes a chain tool. The total cost of your saddlebag should be around $85.

## Bottle Cages and Water Bottles

Proper hydration is essential while cycling. It is a good idea to mount two water bottle cages ($15-$30) on your bike. Water bottle cages usually carry one 12-ounce or 16-ounce cylindrical water bottle with a spout for drinking. The cages are made of steel, aluminum, titanium, carbon fiber, or plastic. Metal cages hold up better to repeated use. Water bottles ($5) vary in quality. Choose those with an easy-flowing spout. The last thing you want while pushing yourself to the limit in the heat is to struggle to drink the water you have been carrying. The benefits of proper hydration and glucose energy drinks are explained in chapter 3 on page 34.

## Bike Computers, Heart Rate Monitors, and Power Meters

Bike computers, heart rate monitors, and power meters help cyclists measure their workload and track fitness improvements. If you are just getting started or are more interested in general health than tracking your fitness and racing, this equipment may not be a high priority yet. However, as your training intensifies, these items may become essential. A handlebar computer measures your road fitness by logging elapsed time, distance, speed, pedal revolutions per minute (or cadence), altitude gain, heart rate, power output, and workload. This information can be a valuable tool while performing your workouts and assessing your fitness, which will be explained later in the book. Sophisticated computers provide the most information but are obviously the most expensive. Simple bike computers are generally priced from $30 to $60 but only provide elapsed time, distance, speed, and pedal revolutions per minute (RPM).

Heart rate monitors pick up the electrical activity of your heart and relay it to the receiver mounted on your handlebar. Your heart rate indicates fitness, fatigue, and effort on the bike. A basic unit that simply measures your heart rate costs about $75. If you get a monitor that tells you the upper and lower limits of your zones and includes speed, distance, RPM, and elapsed time and is downloadable to a computer, you will pay $125 to $400.

Most professional cyclists now train with power meters that measure intervals, power in watts, and work in kilojoules. Cyclists can download this information to a computer for postride analysis that can help them plan their training program. Different power meters provide different levels of accuracy. The cheapest models cost about $700, but they tend not to function well in extreme weather conditions, such as heavy rain, so be wary of lower-priced power meters. Because the technology is new, obtaining accurate, consistent measurements will cost you. Lighter and more scientifically accurate models can cost up to $3,500. Different brands of power meters measure power differently. For instance, the PowerTap brand measures power by collecting data in the hub of the rear wheel and then calculating the power average. The SRM brand collects the data in the crank and then calculates averages. In general, measuring power requires expensive technology but provides the athlete the most accurate and useful fitness information.

# Cycling Clothing

Which clothing you wear while cycling depends on the weather. Always look at the weather forecast before heading out the door so that you are properly prepared for changes in the weather. In hot weather, you can simply wear cycling shorts and a jersey. If you plan to ride in the mountains, you could encounter cold weather, even on a hot day, so always carry extra clothing in the pockets of your jersey. In cool weather, layering is the best way to stay warm. Layers release less heat and tend to wick sweat off your skin, allowing you to remain dry.

## Cycling Shorts

If you ride on a regular basis, you need a pair of high-quality cycling shorts, which are designed to make cycling more comfortable. The smooth padding provided by a synthetic or leather chamois liner does not rub or chafe like the seams running down the center or sides of standard shorts and underwear. Some clothing manufacturers make cycling shorts with a unisex chamois. Others make a gender-specific chamois, which we highly recommend. Men and women have different points of irritation or chaffing and usually are more comfortable with a gender-specific chamois.

Padded cycling shorts are worn without underwear to prevent chaffing and irritation. They are made of stretchy Lycra, and the waist is high in the back so they fit while you are leaning over on your bike. Shorts should cover the leg to just above the knee to keep thighs from rubbing and chaffing on the saddle, and they should fit snuggly to prevent creases that can chafe and irritate skin while riding. If the tight fit of Lycra is not the look you are after, a pair of baggy nylon shorts with a built-in chamois is comfortable for shorter rides. They are not as aerodynamic for racing and may cause chaffing on long rides. Wash your shorts after each use because dirty shorts can lead to bacterial infections and saddle sores. It is a good idea to purchase at least two pairs of shorts so that you always have a clean pair to wear. Prices vary depending on quality. You can expect to pay $35 to $125.

## Eyewear

Sunglasses are essential because they protect the eyes from dirt, rocks, ultraviolet glare, reflections, and insects. The wraparound design of most cycling sunglasses eliminates airflow through the nose bridge and the sides. Many models come with interchangeable lenses designed for a variety of weather and light conditions, from bright sun to overcast skies and rain. Some models even accommodate prescription lenses. Cycling sunglasses are a better option than contact lenses. The wind can dry out contacts while riding, and dust can collect under the lenses. Expect to pay at least $60, and more for prescription glasses.

## Optional Clothing Accessories

The following clothing accessories are optional because they are not a necessity if you are on a tight budget. But if you choose to invest in

© Tim DeFrisco

The right clothes will keep you comfortable on cold days.

them, they will make your cycling more comfortable and could improve performance.

- **Jerseys.** Cycling jerseys are formfitting to improve aerodynamics. Most models contain a blend of fibers that keep you cool in the summer and warm in the winter. The blend wicks perspiration away from your body, which allows the sweat to evaporate quickly. Jerseys are available in a variety of thicknesses and come in short- or long-sleeve versions to provide comfort in all seasons. Layering is a good idea if the weather is cool. You can wear an undershirt under your jersey to help you keep warm. Cotton T-shirts do not make good undershirts for riding because they can become heavy with moisture and reduce the body's ability to cool or warm itself. Instead of cotton, try to wear a wool or polypropylene undershirt that will wick the sweat away. Most jerseys have two or three rear pockets that provide convenient storage for extra clothing, money, keys, maps, a mobile phone, and other gear. Most models have either a full- or half-length front zipper. It is a good idea to buy at least two jerseys so that you always have clean clothes for riding. Expect to pay $35 to $85.

- **Gloves.** Cycling gloves add to your safety because they help protect your hands when you reach out to break a fall, but they also offer performance and comfort benefits. The fingerless design of most cycling gloves gives you a better grip and preserves your dexterity, allowing you to shift and brake easily. Cycling gloves also pad your hands, absorb shock on bumpy roads and trails, and absorb sweat. Expect to pay $20 to $35.

When the weather is cold, long-fingered gloves are a better option. Keep in mind that maintaining control for shifting and braking is a priority; therefore, make sure the gloves are not so thick that your fingers can't function properly on the brakes and gear shifters. A variety of gloves for different types of weather conditions are on the market. These include thin and thick long-fingered gloves and, for extremely cold weather, thick lobster-claw gloves that still allow you to shift gears.

- **Jacket.** A rain jacket provides comfort in cold and rainy weather. To prevent having to complete your ride chilled to the bone after getting caught in foul weather, purchase a jacket that is lightweight and folds easily into a jersey pocket. Expect to pay $40 or more for a lightweight jacket. However, you might also want to invest in a heavier water-resistant and windproof shell, which allows you to keep cycling even when temperatures drop in the winter. The expense for these jackets is normally $75 or more.

- **Tights.** On days when the temperature is below 55 degrees, your rides will be more comfortable if you have a pair of tights to keep your legs warm. This extra warmth improves your safety by preventing muscle and knee injuries, which are more likely to occur on a cold day. If your budget allows, consider buying lightweight tights for cool days and an insulated pair for the winter. Prices range from $40 to $80, with the heavier-weight tights being the most expensive.

- **Arm and leg warmers.** When the weather is too cool to start your ride in a short-sleeve jersey and shorts, wear arm warmers and leg warmers, and then peel them off and pack them away into a pocket as you warm up. Expect to pay $20 to $50 per set.

# CHAPTER 2

# Mastering the Bike

In this chapter you will learn how to choose a frame that is the right size and how to position yourself properly on your bike. You will learn how to pedal efficiently, shift gears, and choose proper gearing while riding—skills that will help you to maximize your fitness and ability. This chapter also discusses the importance of obeying local cycling laws and taking necessary safety precautions while riding, and it suggests exercises that will help you to improve your bike-handling skills, which will increase safety. The chapter ends with guidelines for preparing yourself for each ride and choosing roads and dirt trails to ride on.

## Choosing the Frame Size

Depending on the manufacturer, frame size may be given in either inches or centimeters. The majority of frames are sized based on the length of the seat tube. A good rule of thumb when sizing a road, touring, or hybrid bike is to allow one to two inches (2.5-5 cm) between your crotch and top tube when your are standing over the frame. If you are sizing a mountain or cyclocross bike, you should allow at least two inches (5 cm) of clearance.

Compact frames, which have grown in popularity, are fitted differently than regular frames. These frames have a slanted top tube that is higher at the front than at the back. These are more adaptable than regular frames because manufacturers can fit the majority of body types on just three different sizes—small, medium, and large—rather than the 6 to 10 different sizes regular frame manufacturers must build. When you order a compact frame, the builder uses a conversion chart to place you on the correct size based on your stand-over height on a standard frame. With the proper saddle height, stem length, and handlebar reach, the compact frame can be customized to your specifications.

# Determining Proper Position on the Bike

Correct positioning on your bicycle improves your efficiency and ability to produce power while pedaling. Poor positioning can lead to injury and discomfort and may adversely affect bicycle handling while descending a mountain or negotiating traffic. Several measurements determine a proper fit: frame size, saddle height, knee angle, stem height, and reach.

Measurements vary from person to person and are based on body type and size, the type of cycling you plan to do, and past or current injuries. Bike fitting is done in several steps, so don't expect to *dial in* the perfect fit on the first try. Sometimes it takes a series of adjustments to become comfortable and efficient and weeks or months to develop the proper position. Be patient and experiment by making small changes, testing them, and then readjusting if necessary. You will develop the best position in the end if you maintain patience in fine-tuning.

To maintain accuracy, make all your adjustments to your cycling position with the bike mounted on a home trainer. You will need another person to help with the various measurements. He or she should take your measurements while you are in position on the bike wearing cycling shoes and shorts. Refer to the diagram on page 5 for help finding the various parts on the bike. If you become overwhelmed by the process, you can pay for a professional bike fitting. Check with local retailers for rates and availability. Keep in mind that the quality of the professional bike fit varies from shop to shop. Ask around for input on the best bike-fitting locations in your area.

## Saddle Height

Saddle height is the most important adjustment for attaining muscular efficiency while pedaling. Positioning your saddle at the proper height will help your leg muscles function at their maximal strength, and it will minimize the pressure applied to your buttocks, which will prevent soreness. If the seat is too high or low, efficiency drops, and tension is inappropriately placed on your joints and buttocks.

Set the height of the seat so that while you are sitting squarely on the saddle with your heel on the pedal, your leg is fully extended. This ensures a slight bend in the knee when you have the ball of your foot on the pedal with the crank in the vertical downward position (see figure 2.1). When adjusting saddle height, do not extend the seat post beyond the maximum-height line on the seat post. This line should be clearly marked; however, if it is not, leave at least three inches (approx. 7.5 cm) of seat post inside the frame to provide strength and stability.

**Figure 2.1** Proper saddle-height position.

After adjusting the saddle height, you must adjust the front-to-back position and the angle of the saddle. You will first need to adjust the position of the cleat on your cycling shoe if you are using clipless pedals. The ball of the foot should rest directly over the axle of the pedal. Some cleats allow more rotation than others. Adjust the cleat to allow your foot to be in its natural standing and walking position. If you walk slightly pigeon-toed or duck-footed, position your cleat to accommodate the angle of your foot. Make sure that your heel doesn't hit the crank arm while you are pedaling. While wearing your cycling shoes, sit with your feet clipped into the pedals. With the crank arms parallel to the ground, move your saddle forward or backward so that when you drop a plumb line from the center of your kneecap, the line falls directly to the pedal axle (see figure 2.2). When your knees are properly aligned with the axle, you are able to use your muscles most efficiently while pedaling. Adjust the saddle angle so it is either level or pointing slightly downward in front.

After adjusting your front-to-back saddle position, go back and check the saddle height again. A large movement forward lowers your saddle height, and a large movement backward raises it. Make sure the height is still correct. This is a tedious process requiring multiple adjustments, but establishing the proper position increases comfort, prevents injury, and optimizes power transfer.

**Figure 2.2** Proper front-to-back position.

# Handlebar Adjustment and Reach

Determining the proper reach to your handlebars is based on your arm length, back flexibility, and upper-body strength. Handlebar size (end-to-end measurement), adjustment (level or tilted up or down), and stem length affect the reach. Optimal reach also depends on the type of bike you are riding and the principal type of cycling you do (flat riding, mountain climbing, racing, touring, mountain biking, or time-trialing). Unlike the saddle height, which remains constant on the various bikes, the handlebar adjustment and reach are different on each type of bike.

In general, you want to maintain a position that allows you to ride with your elbows slightly bent at all times to absorb the vibrations and the bumps in the road, giving you better control and causing less fatigue in your arms, neck, back, and shoulders. Adjust your handlebar height and reach so you can ride in this flexed position. Depending on the type of handlebar stem you have, the height can be adjusted by using spacers or simply by loosening and raising the handlebars. Keep in mind that the older style of stem without spacers has a maximum-height line for safety and stability. It is important to make sure you are not supporting too much bodyweight on your hands because doing so can cause numbness in the hands. If your hands become numb, adjust your position by sitting back more on your saddle. This will take some of the weight and pressure off your hands and should help eliminate numbness. You should consult your local mechanic or refer to a repair manual for specific instructions on your model of stem.

Road racers generally try to achieve an aerodynamic position and ride in a more stretched position with the back fairly flat. A road rider usually adjusts the stem height one to two inches (2.5-5 cm) below the top of the saddle, although sometimes climbing specialists use a more upright position that allows them to breathe more easily and pull up on the pedals more efficiently while climbing.

Aerodynamics usually are not a priority on touring and hybrid bikes, so choose a more comfortable upright position on these bikes. This will put less stress on the back, arms, and neck during long rides. On most touring and hybrid bikes, the stem height is nearly level with the saddle height or just slightly lower. A more upright position on mountain bikes helps with climbing, breathing, and maneuverability.

On a time trial bike, strive for the most aerodynamic position possible. This means being stretched out with a flat back and your arms extended in front of the body. A special type of handlebar allows a position that produces maximum aerodynamics. On a time trial bike, you achieve the least amount of wind drag and the best aerodynamics by riding in the lowest position your back flexibility and rib cage will allow.

# Riding the Bike Correctly

Most people learn to ride a bike as children and it seems like a simple exercise once you have mastered balance, but the nuances of proper pedaling technique, efficiency, gearing, and shifting can improve your performance. Additionally, obeying laws and taking safety precautions will increase your safety.

## Pedaling and Efficiency

Ideally, a cyclist should strive to pedal at an average cadence of 90 to 100 revolutions per minute (RPM). This is generally the most efficient range for the muscles and cardiovascular system. However, Lance Armstrong has made riding at higher than 100 RPM his trademark. He credits this high cadence ability as a valuable part of his seven Tour de France victories because riding at high RPM allowed him to conserve his strength and recover better than his competition.

Beginning cyclists tend to push gears that are too big, causing excessively low RPM. This puts stress on muscles, tendons, and joints and may lead to injury. Low RPM cause muscles to fatigue sooner, something we all would like to avoid.

When training at higher workloads, such as riding up a hill, a good rule for determining proper RPM is to equalize lung and leg burn. The goal is for your lung fatigue to match your muscle fatigue. While riding, assess the discomfort in your lungs and your legs. Ideally, these will give you the same amount of grief when undergoing a strenuous stretch of riding. If your lungs hurt more, decrease your cadence (RPM). If your legs hurt more, increase your cadence.

To measure your RPM, you can use a bicycle computer or follow the old-fashioned method of counting the revolutions your leg makes in one minute. In the beginning, it may be difficult or impossible to ride at 90 to 100 RPM. You may feel as if you are bouncing up and down on your saddle as you try. Practice makes perfect. You will become smoother and more efficient with time. If you have problems riding within this range, set small goals for yourself to allow your body to adjust to riding within the desired range. Start off trying to average 65 to 75 RPM, then, when you become comfortable (this may take just a few rides or perhaps a few weeks of riding), raise the range by 5 to 10 RPM until you reach 90 to 100 RPM. Remember that it is naturally more difficult to pedal at high RPM when climbing and easier when descending. If you average closer to 80 to 90 RPM on the climbs and 100 to 120 RPM or more on the descents, your overall ride average will be on target.

Proper pedaling technique will transfer more power from your legs to the bike. You should think about pedaling in circles and distributing power throughout the entire pedal stroke. Many new riders tend to stomp on the pedal during the downstroke. This method is inefficient, causing flat, dead spots in the pedal stroke. Instead, the heel should drop slightly during the downstroke and rise slightly during the upstroke (see figure 2.3). Try to ride with smooth, consistent pressure during the entire revolution of the crank. You'll be amazed at the extra zip you get by pedaling this way.

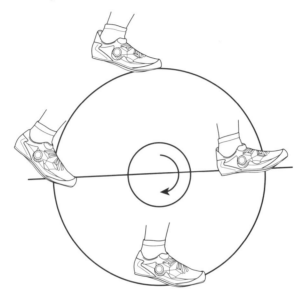

**Figure 2.3**   Proper pedaling technique.

## Gearing and Shifting

Gears are your friend. Just as a car shifts frequently to keep the engine tachometer in the most efficient range, you should shift gears when necessary to maintain a high and proper pedaling cadence. As the terrain, the wind direction, and your level of fatigue change over the course of the ride, gearing should vary to meet the conditions. Cogs of various sizes are located on the rear hub, and chainrings in various sizes are located on the crank of the bicycle. The number of teeth on the cog or chainring determines the size. By changing the combinations of the front chainring and rear cog, you can attain various gearing ratios. The largest front chainring and smallest cog in the back constitute the biggest gear ratio, similar to fifth gear on a manual transmission automobile. It is also the gear ratio that allows you to go the greatest distance with each revolution of the crank. In contrast, the smallest front chainring and the largest cog in the back constitute the smallest gear ratio. It causes the bike to travel the shortest distance per revolution. Generally riders spin bigger gears on the descents, smaller gears on the climbs, and middle gears on the flat sections of road.

If you practice shifting, it will become automatic. Shift to a bigger gear when you begin to "spin out," a situation in which your legs can no longer keep up with the pedals. Shift to a smaller gear when your RPM drop and you start losing momentum. Over time you will smooth out your pedal stroke and use your muscle strength more efficiently. This will save your knees from the stress of riding in a gear that is too big.

## Laws and Safety Precautions

It is a good idea to brush up on local cycling laws if you are not familiar with them. Many regions levy hefty fines for not obeying the law. Bikes are considered vehicles and so must ride with traffic and follow the same rules as automobiles. Some states allow cyclists to ride two by two; others demand that cyclists ride single file. Helmets are mandatory in some regions, not in others. The laws vary from one state to the next. Do not allow yourself or your wallet to become a victim of ignorance.

Being prepared for your rides will ensure that you perform at your best and will make riding more comfortable and enjoyable. The following tips will prepare you for unexpected situations.

- Always take at least one water bottle, no matter the weather conditions or the length of the ride. Drink before you feel thirsty. Dehydration is a common problem for cyclists. You probably won't notice how much you sweat on your rides because the wind evaporates the sweat.

- Carry snacks, such as energy bars, cookies, bananas, fig bars, or raisins—anything easy to digest and tasty. While riding, you burn a lot of calories, and if you run out of fuel, you will *bonk,* or run out of energy, making it impossible to go any farther until you have consumed carbohydrate.

- Carry extra clothing, money, a cell phone, and an ID with contact information in case of an emergency. You never know when the weather may change. A light rain jacket, gloves, and arm and leg warmers are a good idea, especially in the fall, spring, and winter. Money can come in handy if you need to buy an energy drink, food, or a spare tire to fix a flat. A cell phone in your pocket is useful in case you have a mishap or get lost.

- Pay attention to the wind direction when estimating the time for your ride. You'll ride much faster with a tailwind than a headwind. Be attentive and do not become stranded far from home because you started out with a blazing tailwind and didn't realize how far you had gone and how much effort it would take to make it back home.

# Developing Bike-Handling Skills

Bike-handling skills are essential to ensuring safety while riding and will help you perform well. When comfortable and relaxed on the bike, you can maneuver a bike more skillfully and avoid potentially dangerous situations more easily.

To improve bike-handling skills, find an area with little or no pedestrian or vehicular traffic (an empty parking lot, for example) so that you can practice cornering, accelerating, and sprinting without having to worry too much about moving obstacles. For a mountain bike or cyclocross bike, you can practice on a grass or dirt field.

Set up a small loop course where you can concentrate on taking a corner repeatedly and finding a fast and safe line. Try to feel how your bike moves beneath you; think of it as an extension of your body. Keep your upper body relaxed and your eyes focused on the road ahead. Remember that you cannot pedal through corners, so keep your inside leg up and your outside leg extended, otherwise your inside pedal will hit the ground as you lean into the corner. Slow down coming into corners and accelerate coming out. While you're riding the loop, familiarize yourself with the gears on your bike. Shift into an easier, or lighter, gear when you enter a corner and then shift down into a bigger gear while you exit, making sure to select the right gear for your speed and cadence.

Practice braking at different speeds, making note of how long it takes to slow down or stop. Too much pressure on the front brake will cause you to cartwheel head over heels, whereas too much pressure on the rear brake will cause you to skid. It is important to apply even pressure to the front and the rear brakes to ensure a safe stop. It is also critical to brake before entering the apex of the turn and let up on the brakes as you make the turn. Practice getting in and out of your pedals so that when you are on the road, you are ready to click out of your pedals safely at stop lights and intersections.

With each ride you will feel increasingly comfortable. This new comfort level will transfer into different environments, improving your agility and giving you more confidence. Remember, even the most experienced professional cyclist is constantly improving bike-handling skills with each training ride or race.

# Deciding Where to Ride

Knowing how to ride in different environmental conditions is part of mastering the bike. By taking advantage of the ability to ride indoors, outdoors, and on roads and trails, you will maximize your ability to maintain your training program and gain fitness. The information in the following sections will help you make the most of your training in different environmental conditions.

## Cycling Indoors

The cheapest and perhaps the most comfortable way to ride indoors is to set up your bike on a home trainer. Most home trainers attach to your rear wheel skewer and provide magnetic or wind resistance to your rear tire, allowing you to get a great workout inside. Several companies manufacture home trainers that can be attached to your bike with ease. Trainers start at $90.

It is possible to use an ergometer exercise bike, but these require a much bigger investment (a high-quality ergometer costs $1,000 to $4,000). If you plan to do quite of bit of indoor training, it may be worth the investment, but otherwise, most gyms are now equipped with a fleet of exercise bikes. Some ergometers have power meters built in that allow you to track your workout and fitness gains.

No matter which type of indoor equipment you use, you will need a fan and bottles of water for indoor riding. Because there is no airflow when riding a trainer, you heat up quickly and can become dehydrated from sweat loss. Entertainment, such as music or television, can help pass the time while pedaling. Reading is not a good option during an intense workout, as it requires too much concentration and takes away from your efforts.

## Choosing a Road

Where you train will have a huge effect on the type of workout you can accomplish. Seek roads with paved shoulders and minimal traffic. Some regions have excellent bike path networks; however, use caution on bike paths. They are usually open to walkers, inline skaters, children, and dogs, none of which expect to meet a quickly moving cyclist. It is best to do fast cycling training on the road. Local bike shops and cycling clubs are a good resource for information on roads and bike paths. Some shops carry cycling maps. Some cycling clubs conduct regular group training rides that you can join.

© Eyewire/Photodisc/Getty Images

Wherever you choose to ride, pay attention to your surroundings to decrease the chance for accidents.

## Choosing a Trail or Dirt Road

Dirt roads are often an excellent choice when beginning to ride off road. Traffic tends to be much lighter than on paved roads, and riding on these roads will gradually improve your bike-handling skills. Some road surfaces are packed well enough that you can use a road bike, although more skill is necessary if you are riding with skinny tires. Riding on a dirt road is more comfortable on a hybrid, cyclocross, or mountain bike because they absorb the shock of the bumps and provide a smoother ride.

You can ride a hybrid or cyclocross bike on single-track dirt trails, but mountain bikes are better suited for this terrain. When searching for a place to ride, remember that not all trails are open to mountain bikes. In some regions, erosion from overuse is a problem, and trails may be temporarily closed. Trails are usually marked when they are not open and you should avoid them. You can be fined for not obeying the law, so do a little research to find a trail where cycling is permitted. Local bike shops and cycling clubs are a great resource for finding trail information. One last word of caution: Be careful on trails used by equestrians. Horses are not comfortable around bicycles, and they sometimes react wildly, which can cause accidents.

# CHAPTER 3

# Understanding Cycling Training

Whether you plan to race your bike or just want to improve your cardio-vascular health, proper training habits will make the most of your time on the bike. This chapter describes our training philosophy. Following these guidelines will help maximize your training and limit injuries and fatigue. This chapter also guides you through fundamental training concepts, including goal setting, individuality, adaptation, periodization, and workload variables. Finally, you will learn how to track your progress over time. There is no greater joy in training than discovering that what you're doing today is far above what you were able to do two to three months ago. Our goal is to help you make that joy a reality.

## Training Philosophy

Our training philosophy is simple and easy to follow. If you work within our five principles, your training will pay off, you'll feel energetic, and your health will improve.

## Learn to Train Effectively

Every ride you go on should have a purpose and goal. Instead of simply pulling out the bike for a ho-hum ride, determine the purpose for each ride in your plan. That focus will not only improve your mental attitude but also your training response. For example, even if your goal for the day is just to have fun, your ride offers a benefit. Enjoying yourself and maintaining your love of the bike may be part of your master plan, and this fun workout will pay off in your preparation for other, more difficult, training days. Keep in mind that if at any point your riding becomes a grind, it is time to change your workout plan. Above all, your cycling experience should be a blast.

© Human Kinetics

Make the most of your training by setting a goal for every ride.

## Be Consistent in Training

Consistency is the key to success, and a good training plan can keep your training consistent and on track. As you train, your body adapts and becomes stronger. As soon as you stop training, the gains you have made begin to fade; this process is known as reversibility, or detraining. Unfortunately, you lose fitness faster than you gain it, so the more time you spend away from exercise, the more work you must do to regain your previous fitness level. To prevent detraining, you must be consistent and avoid long lapses in training. Most of us have many responsibilities: work, family, travel, and so on. Sometimes riding gets pushed way down the list. Knowing when your responsibilities may keep you from training can help you devise a plan that will limit fitness loss. At times, putting off training is unavoidable, but you should still make every attempt to at least maintain your current fitness during this time. If you had been riding three or four days a week, try to get out at least once a week to help prevent or slow your loss of fitness. As soon as you have time, ramp your training back up to its previous level. Keep in mind that the longer your layoff, the more slowly you need to increase your training in order to prevent injuries or overtraining.

## Rest and Avoid Overtraining

Rest is paramount to healthful living and effective training. The training you do actually damages your muscles. Believe it or not, you become weaker immediately after training. The gains that you make in your training program occur while you are resting after you have completed your ride. During rest, your body repairs the damage from training and ultimately takes you to a higher level. This process is called adaptation. We'll touch more on this later. The following are tips for getting adequate rest:

- Listen to your body. If you feel tired, take extra time off.
- Go to bed and get up at the same time each day (even on weekends).
- Sleep in a dark, quiet, cool, and well-ventilated room.
- Avoid stimulants like caffeine in the hours right before bedtime.
- Avoid alcohol and large meals right before bedtime.

Overtraining occurs when your recovery can't keep pace with your workload. If you don't allow for adequate recovery time, your body eventually wears down and your fitness level falls off. A normal part of training is applying a workload that fatigues your body's systems. It is even normal to occasionally carry fatigue into a new training cycle. However, after these periods of heavy workload, you should plan adequate recovery time into your program. The bottom line is that strength and fitness increase during recovery. So don't sell your rest periods short. They are an important and necessary part of your training. The following are warning signs of overtraining:

- Decreased performance on the bike
- Poor sleep
- Increased pulse rate upon waking in the morning
- Decreased motivation
- Persistent muscle soreness

## Eat a Proper Diet

All machines require energy to accomplish work. Your body is no different, and the food you eat is the fuel it uses. A healthy diet ensures that your body's engine runs smoothly, efficiently, and cleanly. Fresh produce, lean meat, fish, unsaturated fat, and sources of complex carbohydrate, like whole grains, keep the body functioning well. Many diets attempt to steer people away from carbohydrate, but your body uses it as its primary fuel source when exercising. In addition to glycogen, which is the storage form of carbohydrate, your body also uses alternative fuel sources, such as fat and protein. Depending on your exercise intensity, the amount of carbohydrate, fat, and protein your body uses for fuel varies.

Athletic performance, healthful living, and weight loss depend on a proper diet. The myriad fad diets and eating strategies can make proper nutrition seem confusing. Although proper diet is beyond the scope of this book, the following are a few key points you should keep in mind. Meal choices based on nutrient-dense foods, such as fruits, vegetables, lean protein, whole grains, and essential fats, are the most effective for providing performance and good health. Avoid overly refined carbohydrate and processed fat. Stay away from fast food and sweets. Contrary to a lot of recent press, carbohydrate foods are not evil. They are the main energy source for sustained exercise. In the hour immediately after exercise, a meal high in healthy carbohydrate is ideal. This replenishes your energy supply when your body can most efficiently metabolize it.

## Stay Hydrated

It is no revelation that your body loses fluid as you exercise. This fluid loss reduces your body's performance. To avoid dehydration pitfalls, you must be vigilant in replacing the fluid you lose. Replace too little, and you become dehydrated. Replace too much, and you can suffer from overhydration.

Dehydration is the excessive loss of water from the body. An average adult should drink 64 to 96 ounces (1.9-2.8 liters) of water every day. Juice and carbohydrate energy drinks are excellent hydrators as well. If exercising, that volume should increase. Requirements vary with activity and age, but most active people need two times this basic amount. On a hot day requirements can be higher.

While exercising, it is best to drink fluid that replaces some of the sugar (carbohydrate) you are burning. Many different brands of sports drinks exist, and the majority of them do the trick. A good rule of thumb while riding is to drink at least one 12-ounce bottle every hour. If it is hot, increase consumption to a bottle and a half each hour. Once off the bike, continue to hydrate. The initial hours immediately after exercise are most important for replenishing depleted fluids. That's why you see professionals chugging water right after they finish.

## Lance Armstrong's Dehydration Disaster

Lance Armstrong almost lost the 2003 Tour de France, his record fifth victory, simply by failing to drink enough water before the start of a crucial individual time trial. It was an extremely hot day in southern France, and the pressure was on Lance to put time between himself and his rivals in the race of truth—the individual time trial—Lance's specialty.

Before the time trial, Lance warmed up on the stationary trainer outside the team bus. But because of the distractions of being at the Tour and of the media crush, he didn't drink enough fluids and perhaps spent a little too long warming up. He started the race fast and came through the first time checks at a respectable pace. However, during the last half of the race things began to fall apart. He appeared to become uncomfortable on his bike. His teammates, who knew his usual form, noted that his body swayed and he looked ill at ease. As they watched, they became concerned as his time checks showed him losing time to his chief rivals. Could this be the end? Would his Tour victories stand at only four? When he crossed the line, his lips were white, his body gaunt and weak.

At the day's end, Lance had lost 12 pounds (5.4 kilograms) of water and had paid the price of being dehydrated. He was on the brink of losing the yellow jersey and was unsure if his body could recover from such a fluid deficit. It took him several days to recover from this near disaster. Thanks to his tenacity and will to win, he was able to push through the pain and aftereffects of his hydration error. He went on to finish the race strongly and recorded his record fifth Tour victory.

A good way to evaluate hydration status is by body weight. Weigh yourself before and after exercise. For every pound (453 g) lost during exercise, 16 ounces (.475 liter) of water is needed. If you fail to drink enough, you could easily lose 5 percent of your body weight on a hot, long ride. As you become dehydrated, performance drops significantly. A 5 percent loss of body weight can reduce your work output by 8 to 10 percent. Losing more than 5 percent of your body weight can be serious. A loss of more than 7 percent may even require hospitalization. Different people lose fluid at different rates. Don't wait to drink until your riding partner does; grab the water bottle when you need it.

A simple approach for assessing your hydration level is to pay attention to how often you urinate during the day and note the color of your urine. If your urine output starts to decrease or your urine becomes a darker shade of yellow, you need more water. (Keep in mind that vitamin supplements can also make your urine darker.) Remember, thirst is a late sign of dehydration and cannot be relied on to keep up with fluid loss. Other symptoms of dehydration include lightheadedness (particularly when rising from sitting to standing), dry mouth, muscle cramps, and headache.

Although it is important to stay well hydrated while exercising, don't overdo it. Drinking too much fluid can cause the blood-sodium level to drop below normal levels, a condition called hyponatremia. As the body takes in excess fluid, the blood becomes diluted. This causes fluid to shift from the blood into nearby cells, including brain cells. The result is brain swelling. Early symptoms of overhydration include confusion, lethargy, nausea, vomiting, and muscle cramps. These symptoms are very similar to the symptoms of dehydration.

# Training Concepts

You should know a few basic training concepts before embarking on your training program. These concepts are the keys to creating a personalized training program and quickly and efficiently improving your fitness and performance. The basic training concepts include using a goal-oriented approach to training, recognizing individuality in strengths and weaknesses, allowing for adaptation, determining your training workload, and understanding periodization.

## Goals

Defining your cycling goals is the first key to a successful training program. Remember the first point of our training philosophy: train effectively by knowing the purpose and goal of each workout. Regardless of your fitness level, you should start your training program with a clear set of goals in mind. Your goal may be the ability to ride your bike for an hour without stopping, to complete a century (100-mile ride), or to reduce the amount of time it takes you to churn your way up a local climb. Perhaps your goal is to lose weight or compete in a cycling race. The important thing is to have a goal. Once you reach that goal, set a new goal on which to focus your training. This not only works as a motivational tool but also demonstrates improvement over time.

At the outset of your training program, assess your physical fitness so you can establish reasonable goals given your current fitness level. Chapter 4 gives you the tools to determine where you are and how to apply that information to the workouts and programs presented in parts II and III. In addition, you must evaluate your motivation and objectives to help direct your training program. Set physically challenging, yet attainable goals. Create short-, medium-, and long-term training objectives. Write

© Tim De Frisco

Establishing attainable goals and thinking about them during your rides will help keep you motivated.

these in your training journal to hold yourself accountable, and think about these goals while riding. Doing so will help focus your training and make the most of your effort. Set short-term goals for each ride. Your goals, for example, might be to maintain 90 to 110 RPM throughout the ride or to maintain a consistent, smooth pedal stroke. A short-term goal to pursue over a few weeks could be to set a personal-best time on a local hill climb or to maintain a certain heart rate during an interval. A medium-term goal could be to enter a local race or, if you're more advanced, to win a local criterium or time trial. A long-term goal may be winning a national championship. The possibilities for goal setting are nearly limitless. Once you reach a goal, assess your current fitness level. During your training you should always reach forward, and you should use the information from your assessment to formulate a new goal to work toward. Maybe it is time to try to move up in your race category or to enter more challenging and bigger events.

## Individuality

Everybody is different. That's what makes life so much fun. Because every athlete is different, each one requires his or her own training program. Contrary to popular belief, professional cyclists spend the majority of their training time alone. They might roll out of town together on a ride, but as soon as they get to the meat of their training day, they each do their own thing. Not only may you have different strengths and weaknesses compared to riding companions, but you may also respond differently to your training than others do. It therefore doesn't make sense to undertake the same training as somebody else. Sometimes it's easy to get caught up in what others are doing, but stay focused on your own plan and goals. Chapters 11 through 14 outline a variety of programs to help you establish your own training regimen. Mix and match the workouts in this book depending on your goals, fitness level, and time commitment.

## Adaptation

The cardiorespiratory system consists of the heart, lungs, vascular system (veins and arteries), and blood. This system supplies the body and muscles with the nutrients and oxygen necessary to contract. As you train and exercise, your cardiorespiratory system becomes more efficient at delivering these products to your muscles. Over time, you can supply more oxygen-rich blood more rapidly to your muscles. This equates to increased performance and fitness. Cardiorespiratory fitness determines your aerobic capacity, and the larger your aerobic capacity, the longer and harder you can ride.

Your body adapts because of its desire to maintain the status quo, or *homeostasis*. Homeostasis is the body's tendency to remain stable and unstressed. Every time you work out, it creates stress that "alarms" your body. Your body responds by adapting to the stress so that the next time you do the same workout, it will not create as much of a shock to the system. If you continue to place stress on the body by increasing workouts, eventually you become exhausted. To prevent exhaustion, or overtraining, you must rest after each period of training that stresses the body.

An exercise physiologist friend of ours, Dr. Allen Lim, uses an excellent analogy to illustrate the process of adaptation. Imagine that your fitness is like a container of popcorn, and training stress is the flame on a stove. If you were to place popcorn over a flame, the kernels would slowly heat up. Eventually, some would start to pop and become delicious popcorn. These kernels represent the perfect amount of adaptation. If you become greedy and keep the container over the heat in hopes of making more popcorn, some kernels begin to burn, and you lose many of the earlier benefits of heating the kernels into popcorn (see figure 3.1). With complete overtraining burnout, you burn all your kernels and return to square one.

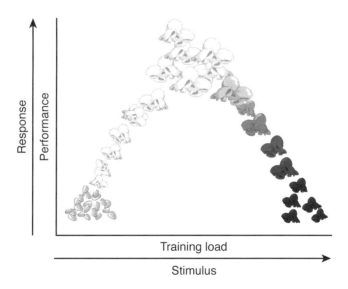

**Figure 3.1** Popcorn: stimulus–response relationship. Applying a training load, or stimulus, in your training program creates a positive response and an improvement in performance. An analogy is placing a flame (stimulus) under a kernel to create the desired response (popcorn). Just as you can overcook popcorn and burn the kernels, you can overtrain and ruin your fitness.

Courtesy of Dr. Allen Lim.

## Workload Variables

Training workload, also referred to as training volume, is the amount of stress you place on your body while training. You can vary the workload in three primary ways: frequency, duration, and intensity. By changing any of these variables, you can increase or reduce the training workload. Let's look at each of these variables individually.

### Frequency

It is easy to understand that the more often you ride, the more stress you place on your body. Riding five days every week is more difficult than riding three days every week if the other two workload variables are kept constant. Sometimes the frequency of rides may not be as important as the duration or intensity. You can use this to your advantage to match your hectic schedule. Perhaps you can only ride three days a week because of work or family obligations. By adjusting the other two variables, you can modify your overall workload to attain the desired result. We know a successful amateur racer who has a full-time career in advertising. He has limited time during the week, so he shifts his training load to the weekend. By arranging his training so that the majority of his workload occurs on the weekend, he has been able to continue excelling at work and at races. Although this may be inadequate training for Michael as he prepares for the three-week-long Vuelta a España, it will be just fine for the majority of cyclists competing in local events.

### Duration

The longer each ride lasts, the larger the training load becomes. When completing rides of equal intensity, a two-hour ride is more difficult than a one-hour ride. In the case of our friend who worked full time and had trouble riding frequently, he increased his load by lengthening his weekend rides. An effective strategy for keeping your workload high is to schedule a long intense ride the day before one that will be overwhelmed with noncycling responsibilities. This technique has limitations, however. You can't go on a six-hour ride once a week and expect the same result as when putting in three two-hour rides. Remember, you need to be consistent and avoid deconditioning, and taking a six-day break between rides will certainly cause deconditioning. But, you can be flexible in the way you maintain your workload. If you know your training frequency will be limited during a given week, you can offset that potential drop in workload by increasing the duration on the days you are able to train.

### Intensity

Intensity refers to how hard you ride, and it is the most difficult of the three variables to get right. Many people feel that to get a good workout, they need to kill themselves throughout the entire ride. This definitely is not the case. Intensity, like everything else in a training program, is just one piece of the puzzle. By varying the intensity level and combining intensity with various durations and frequencies, your fitness will soar.

The intensity level you achieve during a workout is often referred to as a training level, or zone. Depending on the measuring equipment available, these training zones can be based on three different parameters: perceived exertion, heart rate, and power output. Each of these can be used independently or in concert. These parameters allow athletes at all levels to base their training on the same principles. For example, if you are a beginning cyclist and don't own a heart rate monitor or power meter, the perceived exertion scale gives an accurate indication of intensity. On the other hand, if you are a professional training for the national championships, you can use all three indicators to help guide your training. Let's look at each of these parameters in turn.

- **Rating of perceived exertion (RPE).** The numerous intensity scales that are available all do essentially the same thing: quantify your intensity based on how hard you feel you are riding. The key is to set a scale and stick with it. Over time, you will become in tune with your effort and will be able to accurately and consistently rate your training intensity. This book uses a scale of 1 to 10 because it is simple and straightforward. A rating of 10 is the most intense. It signifies the most difficult, eye-popping intensity you have ever experienced. You can maintain this for only seconds, as when sprinting uphill for the finish line. At the other extreme, 1 represents the least intensity. It signifies a leisurely ride: riding along, taking it easy, chatting with friends. Chapter 4 walks you through determining your lactate threshold based on your perceived exertion.

- **Heart rate zones.** Your heart rate is measured in beats per minute. The five heart rate zones are based on percentages of your maximum heart rate, and working in each zone stresses a different energy system. For instance, when working at 60 to 69 percent of your maximum heart rate, you are training your endurance energy system. At 70 to 79 percent of your maximum heart rate, you are training your lactate threshold energy system. You will learn more about training with heart rate zones in chapter 4 as well as in part II.

- **Power output.** Professional and serious cyclists often train with a power meter. These computers are fairly expensive, so do not feel obligated to buy one. Just as you can determine your heart rate at various training intensities, you can also determine your power output in different training zones. Power, measured in watts, is the most accurate measure of how much work you are doing on the bike. By measuring the torque on the crank arm or in the hub, the power meter can determine how much work (measured in kilojoules) you did on your ride. By applying a fairly simple math equation, you can estimate kilocalories from kilojoules. To simplify things even further, this equation roughly shows that, for a cyclist, one kilojoule equals one kilocalorie. Because of the expense of power meters, the workouts in this book rely on your heart rate and RPE. For those who have a power meter, we will show you how to determine your power output at lactate threshold, and you can then apply these numbers to your workouts.

When used together, these three parameters shed light on the finer details of your body's adaptation. That being said, each works well individually. When Dede was training for the Olympics, she used all three to monitor her progress and her training program. If you don't own a heart rate monitor or power meter, no problem. RPE is what you will use to measure your intensity level.

## Periodization

Periodization is the systematic, stepwise approach to organizing your training schedule into various periods, or training cycles. By combining the various training cycles, you will create your overall training program. Generally, a training program looks at the big picture. Which events or goals are primary? Working backward, you create blocks of training that focus on specific aspects that will prepare you for those events. Whether it's to increase your endurance, raise your lactate threshold, or increase your maximal effort (discussed in the next chapter), your program will help you identify and work toward your training goal. Everything flows from your overall goal. The periodization program's purpose is to move you from general fitness to peaking for your predetermined goal or event.

A proper periodization program works through a hierarchy concept. Each day builds into each week, which builds into each month and so on. Because not all training fits into a standard calendar format, a periodization program is broken into different training cycles that build on each other just as days build weeks, which build months. The smallest of the training cycles is called the microcycle. This consists of two to seven days. Multiple microcycles placed back-to-back create a mesocycle. Generally, the mesocycle ranges from two to six weeks. By placing mesocycles back-to-back, a training program establishes the macrocycle, which is the largest training period (see figure 3.2). This encompasses your overall plan. For racers, the macrocycle includes the entire season. Keep in mind that the training plan of each cycle, whether

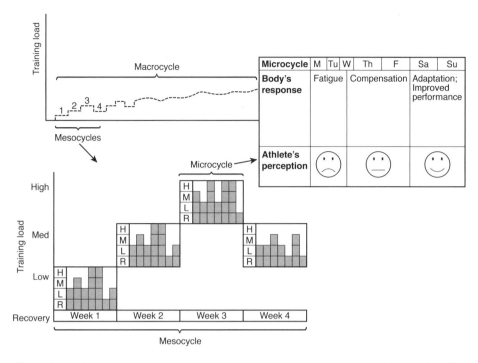

**Figure 3.2** Training cycles. Training programs are broken into various training cycles. The largest cycle, the macrocycle, is broken down into numerous mesocycles. Mesocycles are further broken down into microcycles. Microcycles are the smallest components of your periodization program. Expanded views of a mesocycle and microcycles are shown in the lower graph.

Courtesy of Dr. Allen Lim.

it is a microcycle or macrocycle, consists of overload, recovery, and goal attainment or competition. The length of each training cycle varies depending on your current fitness level and overall goals.

The cycles of a periodization program help establish training goals. One mesocycle may focus on increasing your endurance. Another, later in the year, may focus on developing lactate threshold. Within each mesocycle, multiple microcycles focus on finer points of the more general mesocycle goal. For example, during a mesocycle focused on endurance, the first microcycles might focus on long rides, followed by a microcycle that includes more rest days. The microcycles flow into the mesocycles, which flow into the macrocycle. The overall goal is to establish a base and then move toward more specific and focused fitness. The periodization program gives your body periods of stress followed by adequate periods of rest. Each cycle builds on the previous cycle. Over time, your body adapts to the stress and becomes stronger, fitter, and faster.

The later chapters in this book provide workouts and programs you can plug into your own periodization program. Also included is a blank training program (see the appendix) so you can plan and track your own periodization program. To train efficiently and effectively, you should have a plan that slowly progresses toward your goal. Each training cycle can stand alone, but it should logically flow into the next. When the cycles are placed together, a step-by-step training program comes into focus.

## Tracking Your Mileage and Progress

Keeping a detailed training diary allows you to track progress in training and racing, evaluate successes and failures, and refine future training programs. Your training diary supports and monitors your workout plan. If you use one of the workout programs in this book, you will have a plan for what you should do during each workout. However, your diary will keep track of what you actually did rather than what you had planned to do. After working out for a few weeks, you will be able to look back over the training diary and see how you are progressing. Are you sticking with your program? Are you becoming overly fatigued? Do you feel stronger? After tracking your progress, you will be able to modify future riding and training. For instance, if you found yourself consistently overachieving on your rides, you can adapt your next training cycle to be slightly more difficult than previously planned. Thanks to your training diary, you can fulfill the first point of our training philosophy: train effectively. If you don't keep track of your workouts, you may miss an opportunity to improve your fitness during the next phase.

You can use any basic calendar as a training diary. Some people prefer to purchase a diary specifically for cycling, while others prefer to create their own on a spreadsheet program. Your diary can stand alone or your periodization program can serve as your diary. Both systems work well. Page 47 provides a basic training diary template that you can copy for your own use. Page 47 also provides a sample of how you can use a basic training diary to track your progress.

Regardless of the type of calendar you use, you should record key information daily. This information will differ depending on whether you use the basic diary or the advanced diary. The most basic diary records a few key parameters: how you feel (happy, sad, motivated, and so on), the type of ride you have completed, ride distance, intensity of ride in RPE, and fatigue level before and after your ride. Fatigue can be rated on a scale of 1 to 10. A fatigue level of 1 means you feel fantastic—well rested, fit, and ready to take on the world. A fatigue level of 10 means you're exhausted; you can barely make it from the bed to the bathroom. In your training diary, you will also record your goals and your progress toward achieving them.

Keeping a more advanced training diary requires more time, tools, and effort. Ultimately, you will learn more and be better able to adapt your future training programs using the information you have collected. If you are just starting out in cycling, the basic diary offers you adequate information to monitor and improve your training. If you are more advanced, you will likely want to use a more comprehensive diary; see pages 48 and 49 for a template and sample). You may also include average speed and pedal cadence. If you have a heart rate monitor, record maximum heart rate, average heart rate, and time spent in each heart rate training zone (discussed in more detail in part II). Additionally, if you have a power meter, document the maximum power, average power, total work in kilojoules, and calories expended for each ride. Because sleep is important, include the number of hours you sleep each day. Include brief comments about life stressors and things that are going on outside of cycling. Finally, whether you are keeping a simple or complex diary, keep track of your cycling goals and your progress toward attaining them. This record can serve as motivation and increase your enjoyment of your training program.

In addition to tracking your progress, your training diary also helps you adjust your training so that you peak at the appropriate time for your event. Your whole periodization program's purpose is to peak for your primary goal. After a few months of riding, you will be in better shape than when you began. In training lingo this is referred to as progression, and it is the result of a well-planned training program. When you look back over your training diary, you will see that your body goes through cycles. As you increase your training workload, your fatigue increases. As you taper off after an intense training period, your fatigue will start to drop and fitness will improve. If you graph your fitness and fatigue, you will see two graphs that oscillate in a sinusoidal fashion (see figure 3.3). Like the waves in the ocean, there will be peaks and troughs.

Your goal is to adjust your training so that your fatigue level approaches a trough while your fitness level approaches a peak at the time of your primary goal. This is the concept behind peaking for an event. When Dede won her silver medal in the Olympic time trial, she had timed her training to perfection. She maximized her fitness and came into the race feeling fresh and ready to crank out a fantastic time.

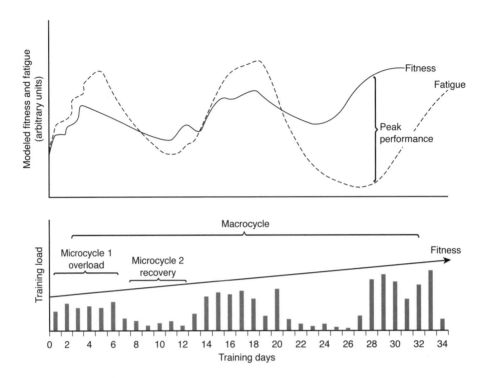

**Figure 3.3** Fitness, fatigue, and the adaptive process. As you train, your body will become fatigued in response to the training load. With recovery, your fitness level will increase. This cycle of fatigue, recovery, and increased fitness continues throughout your training program. Peak performance occurs when your fitness level is at an apex and your fatigue level is at a low point.

# Basic Training Diary

Date _____

How I feel today _____

Fatigue level before riding (1-10) _____

Type of ride _____     Route _____

Time _____     Distance _____

Intensity _____

Fatigue level after riding (1-10) _____

Goals _____

Progression toward goal achievement _____

_____

Basic training diary template.

# Basic Training Diary

Date _July 6_____

How I feel today _energetic_____

Fatigue level before riding (1-10) _1_____

Type of ride _flat spin with sprints___     Route _flat loop_____

Time _1 hour_____     Distance _15 miles_____

Intensity _RPE 4-5_____

Fatigue level after riding (1-10) _4_____

Goals _beat my training partner in all the sprints_____

Progression toward goal achievement _I won 4 of 6 sprints. Not bad.___

Sample of a completed basic training diary page.

From *Fitness Cycling* by Dede Demet Barry, Michael Barry, and Shannon Sovndal, 2006, Champaign, IL: Human Kinetics.

# Advanced Training Diary

Date _____

How I feel today _____

_____

Hours slept _____        Morning heart rate _____

Life stressors _____

_____

Fatigue level before riding (1-10) _____

Type of ride _____        Route _____

Time _____        Distance_____

Intensity_____

Average speed _____        Average cadence _____

Average heart rate_____        Max heart rate _____

Average power _____        Max power _____

Kilojoules of work_____        Calories _____

Time in each training zone _____

_____

Fatigue level after riding (1-10) _____

Goals _____

_____

Progression toward goal achievement _____

_____

_____

Advanced training diary template.

From *Fitness Cycling* by Dede Demet Barry, Michael Barry, and Shannon Sovndal, 2006, Champaign, IL: Human Kinetics.

# Advanced Training Diary

Date __July 6__

How I feel today __I woke up feeling a little tired from yesterday's__ __workout, but motivated.__

Hours slept __8 hours__          Morning heart rate __45 beats per minute__

Life stressors __I have to finish a work project this afternoon that is__ __going to be tiring.__

Fatigue level before riding (1-10) __6 (a little tired from yesterday's training)__

Type of ride __mountain ride with race simulation__ Route __Ward-Nederland__

Time __3 hours__          Distance __56 miles__

Intensity __8-10__

Average speed __20 mph__          Average cadence __90__

Average heart rate __150__          Max heart rate __204__

Average power __230 watts__          Max power __1,200 watts__

Kilojoules of work __2,030__          Calories __2,100__

Time in each training zone __Zone 1: 10 minutes, Zone 2: 62 minutes,__ __Zone 3: 68 minutes, Zone 4: 28 minutes, Zone 5: 12 minutes__

Fatigue level after riding (1-10) __9__

Goals __to average about 300 watts on the climbs lasting__ __15-30 minutes__

Progression toward goal achievement __I averaged 295 watts on the__ __climbs. I didn't quite reach 300 average, but I'm getting closer to__ __the mark.__

Sample of a completed advanced training diary page.

# CHAPTER 4

# Assessing Cycling Fitness

Cycling is a fantastic sport for cardiovascular health. Whether you plan to race your bike or merely ride it for exercise, the health benefits will be many. Before you start to exercise on your bike, check with your physician to ensure that you can handle the added stress of exercise. As you begin your exercise program, start slowly and build over time in frequency, intensity, and duration.

Knowing your fitness level before you begin allows you to properly use the workouts found in later chapters. Every sport requires the use of a specific set of muscles and specific positions, and cycling is no different. Even if you are a fairly active runner or swimmer, you must give your body time to adjust to riding a bike. Initially, your shoulders, neck, buttocks, and legs may be sore. Correct positioning, discussed in chapter 2, will help reduce this. Pay special attention to saddle height, top-tube length (including the stem), and cleat position if you are using cycling shoes. After two weeks of regularly riding your bike, you should start to feel comfortable with your positioning. If you continue to feel pain in a given area, such as your knees or neck, you should probably readdress your position. Your body is highly skilled at adapting to new environments and stresses, so you should look for plausible causes when discomfort is persistent.

A few key parameters, such as maximal heart rate, $\dot{V}O_2$max, and lactate threshold, are used to assess your cycling fitness level and appropriate training zones. Some elite athletes measure these parameters in a laboratory setting with complicated machines and blood tests. Fortunately, simpler techniques can give you a good idea of your fitness level. The remainder of this chapter discusses these parameters and how to measure them for yourself. Once you have this information, the later chapters will help you apply these parameters to your personal training plan.

# Maximal Heart Rate

Maximal heart rate refers to the greatest number of times your heart can contract in a minute. Your heart rate increases in a linear fashion as the intensity of an activity increases. As your workload increases, you eventually reach a point where your heart beats at its maximal rate—at this point, increased workload will not raise your heart rate.

Your maximal heart rate lets you quantify your "ceiling," or maximal effort, and allows you to base your training effort on a percentage of your maximal heart rate. If you don't have a heart rate monitor, you can still gauge your training based on your maximal effort by using the rating of perceived exertion (RPE). When you measure your maximal heart rate, you indirectly measure your body's performance ceiling. Certain laboratory tests can directly measure an athlete's performance ceiling: the maximal rate of oxygen consumption, or $\dot{V}O_2$max. Although you don't need to know your true $\dot{V}O_2$max to train with this book, a further explanation of the term will help you understand your body's physiology and its relationship to maximal heart rate.

$\dot{V}O_2$max is the greatest amount of oxygen the body can use during a sustained bout of maximal exercise. The body uses oxygen to convert food into energy; therefore, the more oxygen you can take in and convert, the more energy, power, or speed you can generate. $\dot{V}O_2$max defines the size of an endurance athlete's "engine," which determines the upper limit of his or her performance. Research shows that $\dot{V}O_2$max is one of the greatest predictors of performance in endurance sports, such as cycling, triathlon, distance running, and Nordic skiing. Unfortunately, finding the next winner of the Tour de France is not as simple as finding the person with the highest $\dot{V}O_2$max. Ability to perform in races also depends on factors such as lactate threshold, which will be discussed later, proper peaking, nutrition, mental fortitude, and tactics.

To better understand $\dot{V}O_2$max, think of two race cars: a dragster with a large engine (high $\dot{V}O_2$max) and a stock car with a much smaller engine (lower $\dot{V}O_2$max). If they raced, which one would win? It depends. If they raced on a quarter-mile drag strip, the dragster with the larger engine would win. However, in a 400-mile race, the stock car, even though it has a smaller engine, would finish first, because although the dragster may be fast for short bursts (maximal effort), it can't maintain this speed for very long. So why is the stock car better suited for a longer race? We'll answer that after discussing lactate threshold.

So how do you measure $\dot{V}O_2$max in the field? Unfortunately, $\dot{V}O_2$max can only be measured through laboratory testing. However, when you reach your maximal heart rate, you most likely are operating at roughly your $\dot{V}O_2$max as well. Therefore, your heart rate provides a cheap and easy measure on which to base your workout efforts. If you want to know your true $\dot{V}O_2$max, schedule a testing session with a sports performance center. Keep in mind that quality varies from site to site; therefore, it is a good idea to conduct research before paying the testing fee of $75 to $150. If taking a laboratory test is not an option or on your agenda, you can estimate your maximal heart rate on your own. Numerous methods have been published, and many of the techniques work well. For the sake of simplicity, we will explain two different methods. The first and simplest method is calculated maximal heart rate. Be aware that results can vary widely using this method, but it is simple and fast, and you can apply the results to your next training ride. If you want to more accurately determine your heart rate and are willing to invest a bit of time and effort, use the measured method. The following directions will help you find your maximal heart rate (MaxHR) using the calculated and measured methods.

## Find Your Maximal Heart Rate

### Calculated Method

You can use a simple equation to calculate your maximal heart rate. Because of the physiological differences between men and women, an equation is provided for each.

Women: 226 – age = age adjusted MaxHR

Men: 220 – age = age adjusted MaxHR

For example, the maximal heart rate of a 35-year-old woman would be calculated as follows: 226 – 35 = 191 MaxHR.

### Measured Method

Aside from going to the laboratory, the measured method gives you the most accurate result. It takes more motivation and effort than the simple calculated method, but it provides much more accurate data.

#### *Directions*

Find a section of road that has a constant mellow grade (it can be flat or slightly uphill, but avoid long downhills or rolling hills). You may also use a home trainer if you prefer. If you have a heart rate monitor, consult the manual to figure out how to record or check your heart rate data. Use the following steps to measure your maximal heart rate:

1. Eat two to three hours before your test.
2. Ensure your heart rate monitor is working properly (if you have one).
3. Arrive at your predetermined testing course.
4. Warm up for 15 to 20 minutes.
5. Start riding at a moderate pace (just to the point where your breathing picks up).
6. Increase your speed by one mile per hour every minute.
7. Reach down deep and continue until you can go no farther.
8. At your maximum, record your heart rate on your heart rate monitor. If you are not using a heart rate monitor, immediately stop and check your heart rate by counting your pulse.

#### *Notes*

When you are at maximal heart rate, a manual measurement of your pulse will slightly underestimate the maximal rate. This occurs because as soon as you stop working, your heart rate slows. Also take a mental note of your perceived exertion during this test. This should represent an RPE of 9 to 10.

Now that you know your maximal heart rate, you can apply it to your training, and part II will give you the opportunity to do just that (see Intensity Levels Based on MaxHR on page 73). As you train, your primary goal is to have your lactate threshold zone increase as a percentage of your maximal heart rate. This means that for a given perceived and sustainable effort you will produce more power and your bike will move faster. Your body has adapted to your training and you are fitter than when you started. Now that we have the first piece of the puzzle, maximal heart rate, it's time to move on to the really exciting stuff: lactate threshold.

# Lactate Threshold

Regardless of the initial energy source—fat, protein, or carbohydrate—your body converts food to adenosine triphosphate (ATP). ATP is the body's energy nugget. It is what your muscles use to fuel their work. When you pedal your bike, the appropriate muscles start to fire and contract. As your exercise intensity increases, more muscle fibers must contract, and as a result you use more ATP. Because your muscles will continue to work only as long as they have an adequate supply of energy, your body uses two primary systems to ensure a constant flow of ATP. During exercise at lower intensity, your body primarily uses oxygen to make ATP. This is called aerobic metabolism. As intensity increases, your body starts to increase ATP production through another system that doesn't require oxygen: anaerobic metabolism. This is where lactic acid comes into play. Lactic acid is a marker of exercise intensity and anaerobic metabolism. As your exercise intensity increases, lactic acid concentration in your blood increases. Your body continually makes and removes lactic acid at all intensity levels, including getting up from your chair. However, at higher levels of intensity, lactic acid production rises.

The key to performance in sport and exercise is balancing the rate of lactic acid production with the rate of lactic acid absorption. During light and moderate exercise, the body can absorb lactic acid more quickly than the muscle cells produce it, so the concentration of lactic acid in the blood remains low. However, as exercise intensity increases, the body eventually is unable to remove lactic acid at the same rate it produces it. This point is known as the lactate threshold (LT). Once you cross this threshold, excessive lactic acid in the blood interferes with efficient muscle contraction. As a result, high-intensity exercise stops: Your power output drops, pain increases, and you must slow down. Many books, articles, and coaches also use the term anaerobic threshold. Although there are subtle differences, you can think of these two terms as synonyms.

LT represents the highest steady-state exercising intensity you can maintain for more than 30 minutes. Recall the dragster and stock-car analogy. The stock car may not have the maximal output that the dragster has, but its engine has better sustained power (lactate threshold) and is able to win over the longer haul. Imagine two cyclists of similar size and condition, Hannah and Jill. If these cyclists were to race over a long mountainous course, the outcome likely would depend on the $\dot{V}O_2$max and LT of each rider. Let's assume Jill has a high $\dot{V}O_2$max and a moderate LT and Hannah has a moderate $\dot{V}O_2$max and an extremely high LT. Although Jill has a higher maximal effort, Hannah can maintain a higher workload for a longer time, and Hannah would likely find herself on the top of the awards podium.

Most coaches and sport scientists consider LT one of the greatest predictors of endurance performance. It is also useful for determining training zones and monitoring the effectiveness of a training program. If you're training properly, LT will improve over time. Improvement can be seen graphically in the shifting lactate curve in figure 4.1.

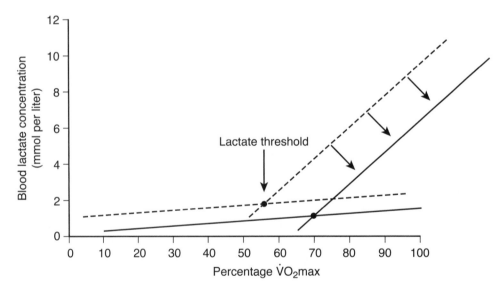

**Figure 4.1** Lactate threshold (LT). As you train, you can move the point where you begin to accumulate lactic acid. With improved fitness, your LT will occur at a higher level $\dot{V}O_2$max. Training will shift your LT curve to the right.

# Find Your Lactate Threshold

As with maximal heart rate and $\dot{V}O_2$max, the best way to find your LT is through laboratory testing. Because this too can be expensive ($110 to $150) and involves multiple needle sticks, we have provided a technique for finding LT that you can use on your own, with or without a heart rate monitor or power meter. Use the following steps to find your lactate threshold:

1. Find a road with a constant grade (avoid undulations or hills) or use a home trainer or stationary bike (but this is mentally tough).

2. Warm up for at least 10 minutes.

3. Ride a 30-minute time trial, trying to achieve your best time. Your pace should cause you the maximal amount of discomfort you can tolerate while still maintaining a constant pace for the entire 30 minutes.

### Without a Heart Rate Monitor or Power Meter

4. Rate your discomfort (perceived exertion) on a scale of 1 to 10 and note your breathing pattern. (Refer back to page 41 for information on rating perceived exertion.) This is your LT. Use this score as a benchmark for your LT. When training at LT, you should feel the same as you did during this test.

### With a Heart Rate Monitor

4. Record the last 20 minutes of your ride. Your average heart rate over this period is your lactate threshold heart rate (LTHR) and is used to determine your LT zone (discussed further under "Zone 3" on page 71). Simply add three or four beats on each side of your LTHR to obtain your LT zone.

### With a Power Meter

4. Record your power over the last 20 minutes of your ride. Your average power over this period will estimate your power output in watts at LT.

If performing this test felt difficult that means you were probably doing it right. When you ride at your lactate threshold, you should be at the point where the pace just starts to become uncomfortable. You go from riding with a friend and chatting, to deciding that the story you were going to tell can wait until you slow or stop. Remember that you can use heart rate, rating of perceived exertion, or power individually or in any combination to train at your LT. This allows your training to be as simple or as sophisticated as you'd like.

# Retesting

You can rerun the maximal heart rate and lactate threshold tests periodically to check your training progress. You can do this once a month to once every three months. To check your progress, complete the test on the same course, under the same conditions, and with the same bike. This will let you monitor your progress and adapt your training. Training is an ongoing process, and over time you will notice fluctuations in your performance. The ultimate goal over time is to see an upward trend in the speed at which you are able to perform these tests.

# CHAPTER 5

# Enhancing Cycling Workouts

To maximize your ability as an athlete, you must take good care of your body. The information in this chapter helps you avoid the common pitfalls of overuse injuries and muscle damage. Included are instructions on how to properly warm up, cool down, and stretch. Unfortunately, even the most cautious and well-trained athletes can sometimes run into health problems, so the chapter concludes with a section addressing common injuries and health issues.

## Warming Up and Cooling Down

At the start of each ride, give your muscles time to warm up before attempting heavy work. Without a proper warm-up, you're asking for trouble. Normally 10 to 15 minutes of easy pedaling will get the blood flowing and warm your muscles; although in cold weather, it will take longer. If you learn to listen to your body, you will be able to determine when you're warmed up and ready to go. Signs that your body is ready can include increased sweating, reduced muscle stiffness, and increased pedal stroke fluidity, but each rider is different. Over time, if you pay attention, you will know what it takes to warm up your body.

Cooling down is equally important. If you dismount the bike immediately after an intense effort, your muscles tighten and your recovery will be prolonged. Five to ten minutes of easy riding at the end of any workout or race will help prevent muscle tightness and help remove exercise by-products that may have accumulated in your blood and muscles. You will likely find that working out is easier and more comfortable the following day if you have done a proper cool down. On television you'll often see professional cyclists dismount their bikes as soon as they finish a race. Do not follow this example. These riders would cool down if they were able to, but they are often limited by crowds, spectators, and postrace commitments. Most of us don't have to deal with these hassles, so we have no excuse not to cool down properly.

# Stretching

Stretching not only protects your body from injury and increases your comfort on a bike, it also improves muscle performance. You can't stretch too much. Before or after a ride and even on days when you are not riding, stretching can refresh, protect, and improve the performance of your muscles. Performing the stretches in this chapter increases the flexibility of key muscle groups used during cycling (see figure 5.1). Cycling uses all the major muscles in your legs, buttocks, and back. Making sure you stretch properly ensures that they don't tense up. Common sore spots include the low back and hamstrings (back of thigh). If you start to feel these muscles tightening, spend extra time stretching them.

Hold each stretch for at least 20 seconds. Don't torture yourself while stretching by attempting to stretch too far, and avoid bouncing into a stretch. Both of these activities can do more harm than good by creating muscle tears that are difficult to heal. Although these stretches help to prevent injury, you may also find that they just feel good and that they relax your mind and body after a solid workout.

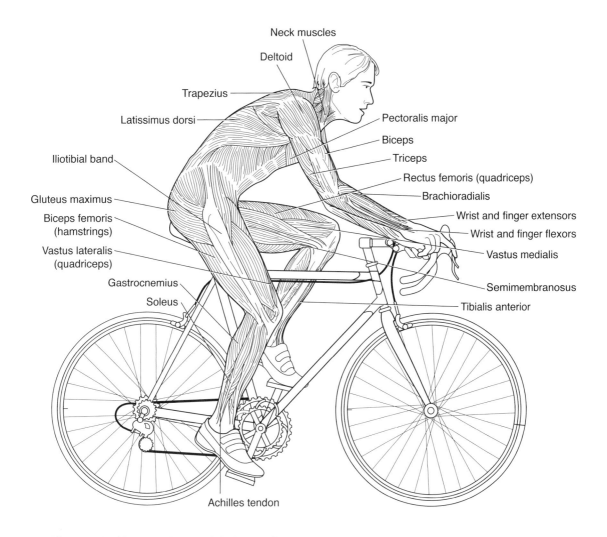

**Figure 5.1** Key muscles used during cycling.

## Quadriceps and Hip Flexors

Stand facing a wall with your right hand flat against it for support. Bend your left leg at the knee and grasp your ankle with your left hand. Push your left foot backward into your hand while keeping the knee pointed toward the ground and your hips pressed forward. Hold this stretch for 30 to 40 seconds. Repeat using opposite leg.

## Hamstrings

Sit on the ground with both legs stretched out flat in front of you. Bend the right leg, with the knee on the ground and the right foot flat against the inner part of the left thigh. Bend down toward the left foot and reach with the arms until you feel the stretch in the back of the thigh. If you are extremely flexible, you will be able to grasp the left ankle with your hands and pull yourself toward the left leg, increasing the stretch. Be careful not to overstretch the hamstring. Hold the position for 30 to 40 seconds. Repeat using opposite leg.

## Hips, Back, and Buttocks

Sit on the ground with the legs stretched out in front of you. Bend the left leg, lift the left foot over the right leg, and place it flat on the ground. Twist the upper body to the left, and place the left hand flat on the ground behind you; place the right elbow on the outside of the left knee. Hold the stretch for 30 to 40 seconds and repeat on the opposite side.

## Iliotibial Band

The iliotibial band (or *IT band*) runs along the lateral thigh from the hip to the knee and is a common location of overuse injuries in cyclists. If not properly attended to, it will tighten and cause persistent pain and inflammation. An extremely tight IT band may not only cause pain over the lateral thigh, but it can also cause hip and knee problems.

To stretch the IT band, stand next to a wall with the right shoulder about an arm's length from the wall. Supporting yourself on the right arm, cross the left leg over the right leg. Push the right hip toward the wall, keeping the right leg straight and allowing the left leg to bend. Your left arm should rest on your left hip. Hold for 30 to 40 seconds. Repeat on the opposite side. You can also use a foam roller (usually available through a physiotherapist or fitness store) to stretch your IT band effectively. Lie on your side on the ground with the roller under the thigh. Slowly roll up and down, placing pressure along the entire length of your IT band. Do this for 30 to 40 seconds, and then repeat on the opposite side.

## Calves

Facing a wall, stretch your arms forward and place the palms against the wall. Position one foot close to the wall and the other two to three feet (0.3-0.6 m) behind you. Bend the knee of the front leg, while keeping the knee of the back leg straight and the heel on the ground. If you can't maintain that position, bring the rear foot closer to the wall. Bend your arms and lean into the wall, keeping your back straight and abdominals tight. Keep the rear heel on the ground in order to feel the stretch in the calf. Hold for 30 to 60 seconds. Repeat on the opposite side.

## Arms and Upper Back

Raise the right arm over your head. Bend the arm at the elbow and grasp the right elbow with the left hand. Gently pull the elbow back until you feel a stretch in the triceps (back of the upper arm), the upper back, and lateral torso muscle groups. Hold this stretch for 30 to 60 seconds. Repeat on the opposite side.

## Low Back

Lie on the ground on your back. Bend your knees and bring them into your chest. Grasp your knees with your hands and pull them toward your shoulders. Hold the stretch for 30 seconds, and then extend your legs slowly, one at a time. You can also do this stretch one knee at a time.

## Low Back and Upper Arms

Kneel on the floor with your feet pointed behind you parallel with the ground. Sit back toward your heels. Bend your upper body down with your arms stretched out straight in front of you. Place your palms and lower arms flat on the ground and tuck your head and face toward the ground. Hold this stretch for 30 to 40 seconds.

## Abdominal Stretch

Lie facedown in the push-up position. Next, raise your head and chest while arching your back. Keep your thighs and palms on the floor. Hold this stretch for 30 to 40 seconds.

# Overcoming Common Problems

If you exercise long enough, you will likely find yourself injured at some point. This section provides descriptions of common cycling injuries and information on how to prevent them and how to treat them when they occur. Having learned this information the hard way, we speak from experience so that you won't have to endure the same problems!

## Saddle Sores

Saddle sores are an issue that cyclists might not like to talk about. They occur commonly, so you'll need to know not only how to decrease their likelihood, but also how to treat them if they occur. Your primary contact with the bicycle is at your crotch, and if you develop saddle sores or boils from uncleanliness, you will become a very unhappy cyclist. These sores usually develop from chaffing and irritation that allows bacteria to enter your sweat glands and hair follicles. As the infection takes hold, you develop a painful, inflamed, swollen sore at the point of contact with the seat. Ultimately the wound matures and begins to drain its contents. Do not attempt to pop the boil or sore by applying pressure to it. This causes the infection to spread to the surrounding tissue. To speed the wound to the point of drainage, apply a warm compress or sit in a warm bath several times a day. Once the wound starts to drain, apply an antibacterial ointment, such as Bacitracin or Neosporin. If you're unlucky or don't take care of your wounds, they may need surgical drainage. If the wound does not improve or if it gets bigger, visit your physician.

The best way to prevent saddle sores is to follow a strict hygiene routine. Clean your shorts with mild soap after every ride. Rinse them well because soap residue can cause skin irritation. Many cyclists use antibiotic chamois creams before each ride to soften the chamois and to reduce the likelihood of saddle sores. Don't lounge around in your shorts after your ride. Remove them and clean your crotch with antibacterial soap and water. You'll be happier if you can prevent this problem before it starts.

## Road Rash

Although we hope it never happens, you will likely experience some degree of road rash during your cycling career. Road rash refers to abrasions and wounds that occur when you crash and your skin scrapes along the ground. The key issue in treating road rash is infection control. After you crash, you must thoroughly clean the wound. First, remove any large foreign materials, such as pebbles and sticks. It is best to clean a wound with aggressive irrigation. However, this may not work if asphalt and debris are stuck to the tissue, so you may have to gently scrub the wound with a soft sponge or brush. Contrary to popular belief, avoid hydrogen peroxide because it will damage the healthy skin at the margins of the wound. This surrounding skin promotes new healing and skin growth, so you don't want to irritate it more than it already is.

For larger wounds, go to the emergency room. The medical staff will likely give you numbing cream before they start to clean, and this is usually worth the copay or treatment expense. The emergency staff will ensure that the wound is thoroughly cleaned. They can also teach you how to properly care for the wound once you leave. Once clean, you should place antibiotic ointment on the wound and cover it with a clean dressing. The best bandage option is an adherent dressing such as DuoDerm or 2nd Skin. You can also use a nonstick pad such as Adaptic and secure it with tape, OpSite, or Tegaderm. Although these bandages are more expensive than others, they are easy to apply and don't hurt as much when you remove them.

## Overuse Injuries

Many cyclists, the authors included, have a tendency to overtrain at times. That is why you must listen to your body and avoid straining it beyond its capabilities. We have recommended that you ease into a training program and gradually build up your time and intensity on the bike. If you find yourself with aches and pains after riding, take a break. A few easy or complete rest days are sometimes all the body needs to rejuvenate itself and avoid a major injury. As a general rule, apply ice to the area of discomfort for the first 48 hours. Wrap a bag of ice or a bag of frozen peas in a thin towel. Apply it to the injured area for 15 minutes out of every hour for the first two days. Don't place the ice directly on your skin; this can cause localized skin damage and frostbite. An anti-inflammatory medication such as acetaminophen (Tylenol) or nonsteroidal anti-inflammatory drugs (NSAIDs) such as ibuprofen (Motrin or Advil) will also help. Don't use NSAIDS if you have a sensitive stomach or have a history of gastric bleeding or ulcers, as they can increase the incidence of gastrointestinal bleeding.

## Positioning Problems

If you have aches in your neck, back, arms, or knees, you may have to reevaluate your position on the bike. If your seat is at the wrong height, your knees can pay the price. Knee pain is common among cyclists and can sometimes be alleviated by adjusting your seat height and position or switching from a fixed-position cleat-and-pedal system to a floating cleat-and-pedal system. Also, if you bend too far forward, your back, neck, and arms may become sore. If you have difficulty finding a position that alleviates your pain or injury, try getting a bike fit from a professional. Remember, whenever you change your position, you must ramp up your riding slowly so that your body can adjust to the changes.

# The Workouts

In the previous chapters, you learned how to equip yourself, find the correct riding position, and establish a baseline for training. You were also given basic training guidelines and ways to keep yourself limber, injury free, and healthy. Now comes the fun part: actually training on the bike.

Part II contains 60 workouts divided into five chapters. These chapters are based on the different energy systems you will use and the terrain you will encounter when training and striving to meet your goals. Chapter 6 contains endurance base-building workouts that will help you build the foundation necessary for the more intense strength and lactate threshold workouts in chapter 7. The fitness foundation built through these endurance and lactate threshold workouts will prepare you for the more specialized interval training workouts in chapters 8 through 10.

Chapter 8 contains hill-training workouts that will help improve your lactate threshold and allow you to climb hills and mountains faster and more efficiently. Chapter 9 contains specific time trial workouts to help you maximize your steady-state speed on flat to rolling terrain. Chapter 10 contains speed workouts that will allow you to reach peak condition by stimulating your fast-twitch muscle fibers and maximizing your high-end and explosive speed. After working through all the different types of training, you will be a complete cyclist with the ability to climb, time-trial, and sprint.

Each workout includes workout descriptions; time and terrain require-ments; recommendations for pace, heart rate zone, rating of perceived exertion, and revolutions per minute; and comments on how to get the most out of your training. The workouts specify time on the bike rather than mileage because, depending on the terrain, weather, and type of ride you're doing, ride time gives a more consistent and accurate mea-sure of what you've done. You can change the total time parameter on any of the training rides in chapters 6 through 10. This allows people at different fitness levels to perform at the training level they need to.

In part III, we explain how you can plug the individual workouts into a training program. The following names and symbols are used to denote the different types of workouts in this part and will also be used in the programs in part III.

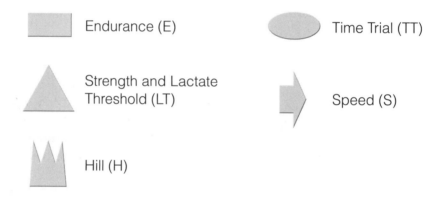

No matter what type of cyclist you are, these workouts will provide plenty of variety to keep you stimulated and motivated. By consistently following them, you will be on your way to becoming ultrafit.

# Understanding Training Zones

Every workout in the following chapters should be performed in a particular training zone. These workouts and training zones focus on various aspects of your fitness and cycling ability. Because you can design a workout program based on either your maximal heart rate or your lactate threshold, each workout lists training zones based on both parameters. Each workout description provides space to plug in your heart rate for each zone.

If you don't have a heart rate monitor, you can use training zones based on your rating of perceived exertion (RPE). It does not matter which parameter you choose to follow, and you may need to experiment to figure out which works best for you. However, remember that as you train and your fitness improves, lactate threshold will occur at a higher percentage of your maximal heart rate, so the absolute numbers in your training zones will change over time.

Different coaches and training systems use various terminology and training zones. This book uses the following five-zone system because it simplifies your training and focuses on the various physiological systems that you must train.

- **Zone 1—Active recovery.** This is the least intense of all training zones and is intended to let your body recover. After intense workouts or training cycles, you must let your body adapt to that training load. Remember that fitness increases come during rest periods, so don't slight yourself on recovery rides.

- **Zone 2—Endurance.** This zone builds a base for your season and future training. During this early training cycle you will spend a lot of time in the endurance zone increasing your aerobic capacity. You will increase your efficiency while riding your bike for longer periods. And you will increase the number of vascular beds and muscle fibers that you will use when you start training at higher intensities in zones 3 and 4. Think of your training like a pyramid: The endurance zone creates the bottom level on which all your training stands. Without a solid base, the rest of your training will fall apart over time. We can't stress enough the importance of a strong foundation. Later, when you start reaping the benefits of your tougher training cycles, you'll be happy you spent time building a training base.

- **Zone 3—Lactate threshold.** You will see great strides in your speed and ability to ride hard when training in the lactate-threshold zone. This is the zone that starts to train your body's ability to delay lactic acid accumulation. By training in the lactate-threshold zone, your body will become more efficient at using available energy and allow you to ride at a higher tempo for longer periods of time. Although this training intensity is difficult, it is also highly motivating and exciting because of the gains you'll notice.

- **Zone 4—Anaerobic.** Training at this high intensity teaches your body to better use your anaerobic energy sources. When your body trains at this level, you produce the unwanted waste products of high-energy metabolism, and you must teach your body to recover after completing a tough interval so you can continue riding. Training at this level will also increase your performance ceiling. You will recall from the discussion on $\dot{V}O_2$max that there is a limit to the amount of work you can do. While this limit is not as trainable as your lactate threshold (as a rough average, cyclists can increase their $\dot{V}O_2$max 10 percent with proper training), noticeable gains are possible. Riding in the anaerobic and maximal effort zones will help you get your pistons firing and take you to your highest possible level.

- **Zone 5—Maximal effort.** Training in the maximal-effort zone not only improves your performance ceiling in the anaerobic zone, but it also trains your neurocoordination when you're fatigued. As you turn the pedals faster and become more fatigued, your form will fall off. By training in this zone, your body will adapt and become coordinated and consistent at a high workload. The maximal-effort zone also trains your ability to sprint and develops maximal power. Think of zone 5 as the tip of the training pyramid.

# Establishing Your Training Zones

You can base your training on RPE, maximal heart rate (MaxHR), or lactate threshold heart rate (LTHR). The instructions in the following sections help you determine your personal training zones using each of these parameters.

## RPE

The simplest technique for determining your training zones is to use RPE only. Use this technique if you are a beginner, don't own a heart rate monitor, or feel overwhelmed by training talk. The following are your training zones if you use only RPE:

### RPE Training Zones

| | | |
|---|---|---|
| Zone 1 | Active recovery (easy) | RPE 1-2 |
| Zone 2 | Endurance (easy to medium) | RPE 3-5 |
| Zone 3 | Lactate threshold (medium to hard) | RPE 6-7 |
| Zone 4 | Anaerobic (hard) | RPE 8-9 |
| Zone 5 | Maximal effort (all out) | RPE 10 |

## MaxHR and RPE

You can also base your training zones on your MaxHR. Because RPE is also available, you can combine your MaxHR numbers with your RPE. The following worksheet will help you calculate your training zones based on the MaxHR you calculated in chapter 4. After you have determined your intensity levels based on maximal heart rate, you can transfer the numbers to the Training Zone Summary on page 75. Then you can refer to this chart for your daily workouts.

# Intensity Levels Based on MaxHR

|  | % of max | | X | Your MaxHR | | HR for zone |
|---|---|---|---|---|---|---|
| **Zone 1** | <60% | <0.60 | X | _____ | = | _____ |
| **Zone 2** | | | | | | |
| Low end of zone | 60% | 0.60 | X | _____ | = | _____ |
| High end of zone | 69% | 0.69 | X | _____ | = | _____ |
| **Zone 3** | | | | | | |
| Low end of zone | 70% | 0.70 | X | _____ | = | _____ |
| High end of zone | 79% | 0.79 | X | _____ | = | _____ |
| **Zone 4** | | | | | | |
| Low end of zone | 80% | 0.80 | X | _____ | = | _____ |
| High end of zone | 89% | 0.89 | X | _____ | = | _____ |
| **Zone 5** | | | | | | |
| Low end of zone | 90% | 0.90 | X | _____ | = | _____ |
| High end of zone | 100% | 1.00 | X | _____ | = | _____ |

## LTHR, MaxHR, and RPE

In chapter 4, you performed the lactate-threshold test and determined your RPE at lactate threshold and your LTHR, so you can now base your intensity zones on LTHR and RPE. Basing your training on your LTHR allows you to target more precisely the different physiological systems each zone attempts to improve. The following worksheet helps you calculate your training zones based on your LTHR and RPE. For easy reference, record your heart rate for each zone based on LTHR and MaxHR in the Training Zone Summary on page 75.

## Intensity Levels Based on LTHR

| | | % of LTHR | X | Your LTHR | | HR for zone |
|---|---|---|---|---|---|---|
| **Zone 1** | | <80% | <0.80 | X _____ | = | _____ |
| **Zone 2** | | | | | | |
| | Low end of zone | 80% | 0.80 | X _____ | = | _____ |
| | High end of zone | 89% | 0.89 | X _____ | = | _____ |
| **Zone 3** | | | | | | |
| | Low end of zone | 90% | 0.90 | X _____ | = | _____ |
| | High end of zone | 99% | 0.99 | X _____ | = | _____ |
| **Zone 4** | | | | | | |
| | Low end of zone | 100% | 1.00 | X _____ | = | _____ |
| | High end of zone | 104% | 1.04 | X _____ | = | _____ |
| **Zone 5** | | | | | | |
| | Low end of zone | 105% | 1.05 | X _____ | = | _____ |
| | High end of zone | 110% | 1.10 | X _____ | = | _____ |

Don't think that calculating your MaxHR will go to waste if you use the LTHR and RPE scale. To track your progress you can calculate the percentage your LTHR is of your MaxHR. By tracking this percentage, you can observe the rewards of training as the percentage increases. To calculate the percentage, insert your LTHR and MaxHR into this equation:

$$\text{LTHR} \div \text{MaxHR} \times 100 = \text{Percentage LTHR of your MaxHR}$$

# Training Zone Summary

| | MaxHR intensity levels | Your MaxHR | LTHR intensity levels | Your LTHR |
|---|---|---|---|---|
| **Zone 1 Active recovery (easy)** | <60% of MaxHR<br><br>RPE 1-2 | | <80% of LTHR<br><br>RPE 1-2 | |
| **Zone 2 Endurance (easy to medium)** | 60-69% of MaxHR<br><br>RPE 3-5 | | 81-89% of LTHR<br><br>RPE 3-5 | |
| **Zone 3 Lactate threshold (medium to hard)** | 70-79% of MaxHR<br><br>RPE 6-7 | | 90-99% of LTHR<br><br>RPE 6-7 | |
| **Zone 4 Anaerobic (hard)** | 80-89% of MaxHR<br><br>RPE 8-9 | | 100-104% of LTHR<br><br>RPE 8-9 | |
| **Zone 5 Maximal effort (all-out)** | 90-100% of MaxHR<br><br>RPE 10 | | 105-110% of LTHR<br><br>RPE 10 | |

# CHAPTER 6

# Endurance Workouts

The workouts in this chapter help you build your endurance and aerobic base. They vary in length from 30 minutes to three hours and should be done at a relatively low intensity level. They are steady rides that help you to build the foundation necessary for the more intense training outlined in the later chapters.

In the initial base-building phase of your training program, most of your workouts will come from this chapter. Then in later phases, you will continue to do endurance rides once or twice a week to maintain your base and to help you recover from the more intense interval workouts.

The workouts in this chapter progress from easiest and shortest to most difficult and longest. If you are a beginning cyclist, take your time in building up to the longer endurance workouts. If you are a more seasoned cyclist, you will be able to build up more quickly. The more lifetime miles you have accumulated, the deeper your overall base. After several seasons of cycling, you should be able to recover more quickly and move on to the longer endurance training sessions more rapidly.

Because endurance riding is not intense, it provides an excellent opportunity to focus on your pedaling technique (discussed in chapter 2) so you can master the art of pedaling smooth circles and get the most out of each pedal stroke. In the comments section of each workout is a focus point to think about while training.

You can do any of these workouts indoors. Riding indoors is a great option in inclement weather or when you can't ride during daylight. However, one drawback to riding solely indoors is that you use different muscles than when riding on varied terrain. To properly develop all your cycling muscles while building your endurance base, it is better to ride on the varied terrain the natural environment provides. Table 6.1 lists the workout times and intensity levels for the various endurance workouts detailed in this chapter.

## Table 6.1  Preview: Endurance Workouts

| Workout | Total workout time (min) | Intensity (HR zone/RPE) |
|---------|--------------------------|-------------------------|
| E1 | 30 | 1/1-2 |
| E2 | 30 | 2/3-5 |
| E3 | 45 | 2/3-5 |
| E4 | 60 | 2/3-5 |
| E5 | 75 | 2/3-5 |
| E6 | 90 | 2/3-5 |
| E7 | 105 | 2/3-5 |
| E8 | 120 | 2/3-5 |
| E9 | 135 | 2/3-5 |
| E10 | 150 | 2/3-5 |
| E11 | 165 | 2/3-5 |
| E12 | 180 | 2/3-5 |

# E1:   Recovery and Easy Riding

**Total time:** 30 minutes

**Warm-up:** 10 minutes of easy riding

**Terrain:** Flat

**Workout:** 15 minutes of easy riding

**Pace:** Steady, easy

**Training zone:** 1

MaxHR for training zone _____

LTHR for training zone _____

**Effort:** RPE 1-2

**RPM:** 90-100

**Cool-down:** 5 minutes of easy riding

**Comments:** The temptation on an easy ride is to go too fast, so be sure to ride like you are taking a casual walk in the park. This ride is meant to be totally relaxing, both mentally and physically. Easy rides help you ease into a new program or actively recover from a hard workout. When you relax on a scheduled easy day, you will then be mentally and physically fresh for the workouts that require more effort. On our easy rides, we like to pedal down to the coffee shop, have a drink, socialize, and then pedal home, or sometimes we simply spin around on the bike paths.

## E2:    Endurance Training

**Total time:** 30 minutes

**Warm-up:** 10 minutes of easy riding

**Terrain:** Flat to rolling hills

**Workout:** 15 minutes

**Pace:** Steady, easy to medium

**Training zone:** 2

> MaxHR for training zone _____
>
> LTHR for training zone _____

**Effort:** RPE 3-5

**RPM:** 90-110

**Cool-down:** 5 minutes of easy riding

**Comments:** Riding at a steady pace, you will automatically go easier on the descents and harder on the climbs. Resist the temptation to push too hard on the climbs just yet. Your goal now is to build endurance. You will get plenty of intensity in the workouts in chapters 7 to 10.

# E3:    Endurance Training

**Total time:** 45 minutes

**Warm-up:** 10 minutes easy riding

**Terrain:** Flat to rolling hills

**Workout:** 30 minutes

**Pace:** Steady, easy to medium

**Training zone:** 2

> MaxHR for training zone _____
>
> LTHR for training zone _____

**Effort:** RPE 3-5

**RPM:** 90-110

**Cool-down:** 5 minutes of easy riding

**Comments:** Remember to pedal smooth circles. Focus on pulling up and pushing down with each pedal stroke. This will maximize your efficiency.

# E4:　Endurance Training

**Total time:** 60 minutes

**Warm-up:** 10 minutes of easy riding

**Terrain:** Flat to rolling hills

**Workout:** 45 minutes

**Pace:** Steady, easy to medium

**Training zone:** 2

> MaxHR for training zone _____
>
> LTHR for training zone _____

**Effort:** RPE 3-5

**RPM:** 90-110

**Cool-down:** 5 minutes of easy riding

**Comments:** Remember to keep pedaling on the descents rather than just coasting; this will help to smooth out your pedal stroke. You will find it hard sometimes to keep up with the pedals on steep descents, but with practice, you will become more efficient and be able to pedal at high RPM. If the downhill is simply too steep for you to pedal comfortably, try to concentrate on tucking to improve your aerodynamic position to gain maximum speed while coasting down the hill.

# E5:   Endurance Training

**Total time:** 75 minutes

**Warm-up:** 10 minutes of easy riding

**Terrain:** Flat to rolling hills

**Workout:** 60 minutes

**Pace:** Steady, easy to medium

**Training zone:** 2

>        MaxHR for training zone _____
>
>        LTHR for training zone _____

**Effort:** RPE 3-5

**RPM:** 90-110

**Cool-down:** 5 minutes of easy riding

**Comments:** As your endurance rides become longer, remember to drink water and glucose recovery drinks. This will help you stay hydrated and ride faster with less effort.

## E6:   Endurance Training

**Total time:** 90 minutes

**Warm-up:** 10 minutes of easy riding

**Terrain:** Flat to rolling hills

**Workout:** 75 minutes

**Pace:** Steady, easy to medium

**Training zone:** 2

> MaxHR for training zone _____
>
> LTHR for training zone _____

**Effort:** RPE 3-5

**RPM:** 90-110

**Cool-down:** 5 minutes of easy riding

**Comments:** To become comfortable on the climbs, stand up out of the saddle and feel the bike move from side to side beneath you. The French call this style of riding *en danseuse,* which means "as a dancer," because the swaying motion of the rider and the bike resemble dancing.

## E7: Endurance Training

**Total time:** 105 minutes

**Warm-up:** 10 minutes of easy riding

**Terrain:** Flat to rolling hills

**Workout:** 90 minutes

**Pace:** Steady, easy to medium

**Training zone:** 2

       MaxHR for training zone _____

       LTHR for training zone _____

**Effort:** RPE 3-5

**RPM:** 90-110

**Cool-down:** 5 minutes of easy riding

**Comments:** Now, we are getting close to the two-hour threshold. Be sure to pack along a little food just in case you suddenly get hungry while out riding. Cookies, an energy bar, or a banana are all good options.

## E8: Endurance Training

**Total time:** 120 minutes

**Warm-up:** 10 minutes of easy riding

**Terrain:** Flat to rolling hills

**Workout:** 105 minutes

**Pace:** Steady, easy to medium

**Training zone:** 2

MaxHR for training zone _____

LTHR for training zone _____

**Effort:** RPE 3-5

**RPM:** 90-110

**Cool-down:** 5 minutes of easy riding

**Comments:** A two-hour ride is a solid effort, and you should feel pretty good about yourself when you get home and put your legs up. Often the day before big races, such as the World Championships or a World Cup, we will do a ride similar to this one with a few steady efforts in zones 2 and 3.

# E9:   Endurance Training

**Total time:** 135 minutes

**Warm-up:** 10 minutes of easy riding

**Terrain:** Flat to rolling hills

**Workout:** 120 minutes

**Pace:** Steady, easy to medium

**Training zone:** 2

> MaxHR for training zone _____
>
> LTHR for training zone _____

**Effort:** RPE 3-5

**RPM:** 90-110

**Cool-down:** 5 minutes of easy riding

**Comments:** Endurance rides are great to enjoy with a friend or a group of friends. It is a good time to cruise along and chat, while making sure you are still putting in the effort you need to without poking along. Many of our most memorable moments cycling have been while riding with each other chatting and enjoying an adventure.

## E10:   Endurance Training

**Total time:** 150 minutes

**Warm-up:** 10 minutes of easy riding

**Terrain:** Flat to rolling hills

**Workout:** 135 minutes

**Pace:** Steady, easy to medium

**Training zone:** 2

>   MaxHR for training zone _____

>   LTHR for training zone _____

**Effort:** RPE 3-5

**RPM:** 90-110

**Cool-down:** 5 minutes of easy riding

**Comments:** In more than two hours you can cover some great terrain. Pull out a reliable map, plan a route, pack the map along with you on the ride, and head out for a new adventure. Each time we get to a new city or country, no matter where in the world, the first thing we do is get a map. From our bikes we have seen many roads even the locals didn't know existed. Lance Armstrong is known for planning his rides each morning, making sure to find the most interesting roads.

# E11:  Endurance Training

**Total time:** 165 minutes

**Warm-up:** 10 minutes of easy riding

**Terrain:** Flat to rolling hills

**Workout:** 150 minutes

**Pace:** Steady, easy to medium

**Training zone:** 2

MaxHR for training zone _____

LTHR for training zone _____

**Effort:** RPE 3-5

**RPM:** 90-110

**Cool-down:** 5 minutes of easy riding

**Comments:** When the rides are close to three hours, it is a good idea to bring along food in your pockets. You might also want to stop to get water along the way because one or two bottles of fluid will probably not be enough.

## E12:    Endurance Training

**Total time:** 180 minutes

**Warm-up:** 10 minutes of easy riding

**Terrain:** Flat to rolling hills

**Workout:** 165 minutes

**Pace:** Steady, easy to medium

**Training zone:** 2

        MaxHR for training zone _____

        LTHR for training zone _____

**Effort:** RPE 3-5

**RPM:** 90-110

**Cool-down:** 5 minutes of easy riding

**Comments:** A three-hour ride is a big accomplishment. You should feel tired from the pedaling but energized mentally by the accomplishment. Eat a good meal with carbohydrate when you get home from your ride to make sure you recover properly.

# CHAPTER 7

# Strength and Lactate Threshold Workouts

The workouts in chapter 6 were steady-state, low-intensity efforts, which build your endurance base. After 4 to 12 weeks of base building you will be ready to step up your intensity a notch and begin building strength and improving your lactate threshold (LT) by doing the workouts in this chapter at medium to hard intensity.

The purpose of these workouts is to build your cycling-specific muscular strength and train your LT energy system so you can average higher speeds (and power output) during your steady-state cycling efforts. These workouts begin with strength-building efforts, which are done at low RPM in a big gear and then move on to lactate threshold efforts in zone 3. When you plan your training program you will include both the strength and lactate threshold training sessions in the same three- to four-week training phase. You will then phase out strength training, but continue threshold training in the following phases to maintain the fitness of your LT energy system. The strength and LT gains that you make will further build your fitness foundation. You will be able to push more watts for a longer period of time. Once your LT is trained, your muscles will be prepared for the more intense race-paced climbing, time-trialing, and sprinting workouts outlined in chapters 8 through 10. Table 7.1 lists the workout times and interval intensity levels for the various strength and lactate threshold workouts detailed in this chapter.

## Table 7.1   Preview: Strength and Lactate Threshold Workouts

| Workout | Total workout time (min) | Intensity (HR zone/RPE) |
|---------|--------------------------|-------------------------|
| LT1 | 25 | 2-3/3-7 |
| LT2 | 40 | 3/6-7 |
| LT3 | 55 | 3/5-7 |
| LT4 | 40 | 3/5-7 |
| LT5 | 60 | 3/5-7 |
| LT6 | 75 | 2-3/3-7 |
| LT7 | 30 | 3/6-7 |
| LT8 | 35 | 3/6-7 |
| LT9 | 50 | 3/6-7 |
| LT10 | 60 | 3/6-7 |
| LT11 | 70 | 3/6-7 |
| LT12 | 85 | 3/6-7 |

# LT1: Strength Building

**Total time:** 25 minutes

**Warm-up:** 10 minutes of easy riding

**Terrain:** Uphill long, steady grade, or on an indoor trainer at high tension

**Workout:** 10 minutes uphill or on the indoor trainer

**Pace:** Steady, high tension on the pedals, medium

**Training zone:** 2-3

      MaxHR for training zone _____

      LTHR for training zone _____

**Effort:** RPE 3-7

**RPM:** 55-60

**Cool-down:** 5 minutes of easy pedaling down the hill or on the trainer

**Comments:** This workout builds strength. Pedaling at 55 to 60 RPM means that you are pushing the pedals with tension. Remember to focus on your pedaling technique: Pedal circles, and keep your head up and upper body completely relaxed. All the power should come from your legs and core.

## LT2:   Strength Building

**Total time:** 40 minutes

**Warm-up:** 10 minutes of easy riding

**Terrain:** Uphill long, steady grade, or on an indoor trainer at high tension

**Workout:** 2 × 10 minutes with 5 minutes of easy spinning downhill between intervals

**Pace:** Steady, high tension on the pedals, medium

**Training zone during intervals:** 3

        MaxHR for training zone _____

        LTHR for training zone _____

**Training zone during recovery:** 2

        MaxHR for training zone _____

        LTHR for training zone _____

**Effort:** RPE 6-7 during intervals, RPE 3-5 during recovery

**RPM:** 55-60 during intervals, 100-110 during recovery

**Cool-down:** 5 minutes of easy riding

**Comments:** It is important to fully recover between the two intervals. Make sure you spin at high RPM in a low gear to keep the circulation in your legs high and to aid recovery.

## LT3: Strength Building

**Total time:** 55 minutes

**Warm-up:** 10 minutes of easy riding

**Terrain:** Uphill long, steady grade, or on an indoor trainer at high tension

**Workout:** 3 × 10 minutes with 5 minutes of easy spinning downhill between intervals

**Pace:** Steady, high tension on the pedals, medium

**Training zone during intervals:** 3

> MaxHR for training zone _____
>
> LTHR for training zone _____

**Training zone during recovery:** 2

> MaxHR for training zone _____
>
> LTHR for training zone _____

**Effort:** RPE 5-7 during intervals, RPE 3-5 during recovery

**RPM:** 55-60 during intervals, 100-110 during recovery

**Cool-down:** 5 minutes of easy riding

**Comments:** After these workouts your legs should be achy from the efforts. This is a good sign. Your engine is growing stronger, and after some recovery you will adapt to the increased workload. Although short-term muscle aches are a good thing, if you continue to ache for more than two to three days, you may be overworking yourself and will need to take some extra time off.

# LT4:   Strength and Lactate Threshold Building

**Total time:** 40 minutes

**Warm-up:** 10 minutes of easy riding

**Terrain:** Uphill long, steady grade

**Workout:** 2 × 10 minutes, alternating between 2 minutes at 60 RPM and 2 minutes at 100 RPM for the duration of each interval, with 5 minutes of easy spinning downhill between intervals

**Pace:** Staccato, alternating between medium and hard

**Training zone during intervals:** 3

>     MaxHR for training zone _____

>     LTHR for training zone _____

**Training zone during recovery:** 1

>     MaxHR for training zone _____

>     LTHR for training zone _____

**Effort:** RPE 5-7 during intervals, RPE 1-2 during recovery

**RPM:** 60 and 100 during intervals, 90-110 during recovery

**Cool-down:** 5 minutes of easy riding

**Comments:** When preparing for the racing season we often do similar intervals where we alternate RPM while riding at a steady pace at our lactate threshold. Doing these intervals is one of the most important things you can do in an effort to become a stronger cyclist. The change in RPM is essential for adaptation. You don't want to become a diesel sedan, but rather a high-octane sports car that can handle varying terrain and can accelerate quickly when necessary.

## LT5: Strength and Lactate Threshold Building

**Total time:** 60 minutes

**Warm-up:** 10 minutes of easy riding

**Terrain:** Uphill long, steady grade

**Workout:** 2 × 20 minutes, alternating between 2 minutes at 60 RPM and 2 minutes at 100 RPM for the duration of each interval, with 5 minutes of easy spinning downhill between intervals

**Pace:** Staccato, alternating between medium and hard

**Training zone during intervals:** 3

       MaxHR for training zone _____

       LTHR for training zone _____

**Training zone during recovery:** 1

       MaxHR for training zone _____

       LTHR for training zone _____

**Effort:** RPE 5-7 during intervals, RPE 1-2 during recovery

**RPM:** 60 and 100 during intervals, 90-110 during recovery

**Cool-down:** 5 minutes of easy riding

**Comments:** Stay focused during these intervals. Keep your eyes on the road ahead, concentrate on breathing in and out efficiently, and stay focused on the effort. You will quickly notice that focusing and relaxing as much as possible allows you to ride faster.

# LT6: Strength and Lactate Threshold Building

**Total time:** 75 minutes

**Warm-up:** 10 minutes of easy riding

**Terrain:** Uphill long, steady grade

**Workout:** 6 × 10 minutes, alternating between 5 minutes at 55-60 RPM and 5 minutes at 90-100 RPM for the duration of each interval, continuing uphill throughout the workout

**Pace:** Staccato, alternating between medium and hard

**Training zone:** 2-3

       MaxHR for training zone _____

       LTHR for training zone _____

**Effort:** RPE 3-7

**RPM:** 55-60 and 90-100

**Cool-down:** 5 minutes of easy riding

**Comments:** Although the workouts in this chapter that build strength and increase lactate threshold are shorter than most of the endurance rides, you are putting out more watts (power) and therefore burning more calories. During these lactate threshold intervals, be sure to eat and drink a little between the intervals so that you can sustain enough power for a proper workout.

## LT7:   Lactate Threshold Building

**Total time:** 30 minutes

**Warm-up:** 10 minutes of easy riding

**Terrain:** Uphill long, steady grade, or on an indoor trainer

**Workout:** 15 minutes

**Pace:** Steady, hard

**Training zone:** 3

      MaxHR for training zone _____

      LTHR for training zone _____

**Effort:** RPE 6-7

**RPM:** 80-100

**Cool-down:** 5 minutes of easy riding

**Comments:** Lactate threshold intervals, if done at the proper intensity, will not feel so tough in the first few minutes, but the fatigue will build through the workout. It is important to focus on maintaining a steady effort throughout. As you fatigue, you must push to sustain your pace.

## LT8: Lactate Threshold Building

**Total time:** 35 minutes

**Warm-up:** 10 minutes of easy riding

**Terrain:** Uphill long, steady grade, or on an indoor trainer

**Workout:** 20 minutes

**Pace:** Steady, hard

**Training zone:** 3

       MaxHR for training zone _____

       LTHR for training zone _____

**Effort:** RPE 6-7

**RPM:** 80-90

**Cool-down:** 5 minutes of easy riding

**Comments:** As you accumulate time at your threshold, the efforts will seem a little easier even though they are becoming more physically intense. This means that you have adapted and your body and mind can now handle the increased workload.

# LT9: Lactate Threshold Building

**Total time:** 50 minutes

**Warm-up:** 10 minutes of easy riding

**Terrain:** Uphill long, steady grade, or on an indoor trainer

**Workout:** 2 × 15 minutes with 5 minutes of easy spinning downhill between intervals

**Pace:** Steady, hard

**Training zone during intervals:** 3

> MaxHR for training zone _____
>
> LTHR for training zone _____

**Training zone during recovery:** 1

> MaxHR for training zone _____
>
> LTHR for training zone _____

**Effort:** RPE 6-7 during intervals, RPE 1-2 during recovery

**RPM:** 80-100 during intervals, 100-110 during recovery

**Cool-down:** 5 minutes of easy riding

**Comments:** Because you will sweat and burn a lot of calories during this workout, you must maintain your hydration and glucose levels in order to sustain your pace. So make sure you drink water or a glucose drink between sets.

# LT10: Lactate Threshold Building

**Total time:** 60 minutes

**Warm-up:** 10 minutes of easy riding

**Terrain:** Uphill long, steady grade, or on an indoor trainer

**Workout:** 2 × 20 minutes with 5 minutes of easy spinning downhill between intervals

**Pace:** Steady, hard

**Training zone during intervals:** 3

       MaxHR for training zone _____

       LTHR for training zone _____

**Training zone during recovery:** 1

       MaxHR for training zone _____

       LTHR for training zone _____

**Effort:** RPE 6-7 during intervals, RPE 1-2 during recovery

**RPM:** 80-95 during intervals, 100-110 during recovery

**Cool-down:** 5 minutes of easy riding

**Comments:** Focus on your pedaling technique, because it will help you to maximize your wattage output and speed at this workload. Pedal smooth circles, even when you are becoming fatigued in the final minutes of the workout.

# LT11: Lactate Threshold Building

**Total time:** 70 minutes

**Warm-up:** 10 minutes of easy riding

**Terrain:** Uphill long, steady grade, or on an indoor trainer

**Workout:** 3 × 15 minutes with 5 minutes of easy spinning downhill between intervals

**Pace:** Steady, hard

**Training zone during intervals:** 3

       MaxHR for training zone _____

       LTHR for training zone _____

**Training zone during recovery:** 1

       MaxHR for training zone _____

       LTHR for training zone _____

**Effort:** RPE 6-7 during intervals, RPE 1-2 during recovery

**RPM:** 80-95 during intervals, 100-110 during recovery

**Cool-down:** 5 minutes of easy riding

**Comments:** Three LT intervals are a lot, and maintaining your effort requires mental focus from the start of the workout to the finish. Think about pulling up and pushing down on the pedals with each stroke and keeping your upper body steady and relaxed. Breathe in and out deeply and rhythmically.

# LT12: Lactate Threshold Building

**Total time:** 85 minutes

**Warm-up:** 10 minutes easy riding

**Terrain:** Uphill long, steady grade, or on an indoor trainer

**Workout:** 3 × 20 minutes with 5 minutes of easy spinning downhill between intervals

**Pace:** Steady, hard

**Training zone during intervals:** 3

        MaxHR for training zone _____

        LTHR for training zone _____

**Training zone during recovery:** 1

        MaxHR for training zone _____

        LTHR for training zone _____

**Effort:** RPE 6-7 during intervals, RPE 1-2 during recovery

**RPM:** 80-95 during intervals, 100-110 during recovery

**Cool-down:** 5 minutes of easy riding

**Comments:** The fatigue of this workout will build. The final interval will most likely feel very difficult to complete. You will dip deep into your carbohydrate stores, and it will be necessary to replace them as much as possible on the bike with glucose drinks and off the bike with snacks and a meal high in complex carbohydrate.

# CHAPTER 8

# Hill Workouts

After three to four weeks of strength and lactate threshold training, you will be ready to raise your intensity another notch. The hill-training workouts in this chapter are to be done at a hard or very hard intensity level. They are race-pace efforts on hills or in the mountains. The intervals in these workouts are generally shorter (90 seconds-10 minutes) and more intense (zone 4 or 5) than the strength and anaerobic threshold intervals.

These more intense efforts work your climbing-specific muscles, helping you build toward peak climbing fitness and preparing you for climbing races or hilly events. The workouts are generally organized according to the length of the intervals: going from longer, hard intervals to shorter, very hard intervals, with race simulation workouts at the end. Completing the workouts in this order will help you build toward a fitness peak. As you near your peak, the duration of intervals decreases and the intensity increases.

If you live in a flat region, you may need to be creative in finding the right place to do your hill workouts. Highway overpasses and parking structures are often big enough inclines for short hill intervals. For the longer hill intervals try riding into the wind. Dede grew up in Milwaukee, Wisconsin, where there are not any hills over 300 meters in length, so she used to do longer intervals into the wind and this prepared her to compete against the mountain goats from Colorado.

The workouts start with a 30-minute hill-training fitness test, that you can use as a gauge of your fitness. Dede and Michael do a hill-training fitness test monthly to measure their improvements. The workouts are arranged in order from the longest intervals to the shortest. They are to generally be done in succession, as when you are building toward your peak, you need to decrease the length of the intervals, but increase the intensity. Although these workouts are extremely intense, they can be done by any level of rider. If you are a beginning or intermediate rider, pay attention to your sensations while doing the workout. If you feel like you have reached the point of total exhaustion, you have done plenty of work, and it may be time to shorten the workout by reducing the number of intervals. Table 8.1 lists the workout times and interval intensity levels for the various hill-training workouts detailed in this chapter.

## Table 8.1   Preview: Hill-Training Workouts

| Workout | Total workout time (min) | Intensity (HR zone/RPE) |
|---|---|---|
| H1 | 50 | 4/8-9 |
| H2 | 55 | 4/8-9 |
| H3 | 55 | 4/8-9 and 5/10 |
| H4 | 45 | 4/8-9 |
| H5 | 35 | 4/8-9 and 2/3-5 |
| H6 | 65 | 4/8-9 and 2/3-5 |
| H7 | 59 | 4-5/8-10 |
| H8 | 54-72 | 4-5/8-10 |
| H9 | approx. 36 | 5/10 |
| H10 | approx. 40 | 5/9-10 |
| H11 | approx. 50 | 5/10 |
| H12 | approx. 55 | 2/3-5 and 5/10 |

# H1:    Hill-Training Fitness Test

**Total time:** 50 minutes

**Warm-up:** 15 minutes of easy riding

**Terrain:** Uphill long, steady grade, or on an indoor trainer

**Workout:** 30 minutes

**Pace:** Steady, very hard

**Training zone:** 4

> MaxHR for training zone _____
>
> LTHR for training zone _____

**Effort:** RPE 8-9

**RPM:** 80-95

**Cool-down:** 5 minutes of easy riding

**Comments:** This is a fitness test, and you can use your heart rate and wattage output from this test to pace yourself in future workouts. You should eat three hours before this workout so that your meal is completely digested. Ride as hard as you can for 30 minutes, but make sure you ride at a pace you can sustain for 30 minutes. If you sprint at the start, you may blow up and be unable to finish. Pick a course that you can reuse. That way you will not only be able to gauge your fitness gains by monitoring your wattage but also by monitoring the distance covered in 30 minutes, provided that the weather conditions are similar each time you do the test.

## H2:   Hill Training

**Total time:** 55 minutes

**Warm-up:** 10 minutes of easy riding

**Terrain:** Uphill long, steady grade, or on an indoor trainer

**Workout:** 3 × 10 minutes with 5 minutes of easy spinning downhill between intervals

**Pace:** Steady, hard to very hard

**Training zone during intervals:** 4

        MaxHR for training zone _____

        LTHR for training zone _____

**Training zone during recovery:** 1

        MaxHR for training zone _____

        LTHR for training zone _____

**Effort:** RPE 8-9 during intervals, RPE 1-2 during recovery

**RPM:** 80-95 during intervals, 100-110 during recovery

**Cool-down:** 5 minutes of easy riding

**Comments:** These intervals are steady efforts at the maximum effort level you can sustain for 10 minutes. If you are training with a power meter, you will notice that your average wattage level may drop from the first interval to the third as you fatigue, but as your fitness improves over time, you will be able to better sustain your average wattage from the first to the last interval.

# H3:    Hill Training

**Total time:** 55 minutes

**Warm-up:** 10 minutes of easy riding

**Terrain:** Uphill 3-7 percent grade, or on an indoor trainer

**Workout:** 3 × 10 minutes, the first 8 minutes at a hard pace and the final 2 minutes all-out, with 5 minutes of easy spinning downhill between intervals

**Pace:** Steady, hard to all-out

### Training zone during first 8 minutes: 4

   MaxHR for training zone _____

   LTHR for training zone _____

### Training zone during final 2 minutes: 5

   MaxHR for training zone _____

   LTHR for training zone _____

### Training zone during recovery: 1

   MaxHR for training zone _____

   LTHR for training zone _____

**Effort:** RPE 8-9 during work in zone 4, RPE 10 during work in zone 5, RPE 1-2 during recovery

**RPM:** 80-95 during intervals, 100-110 during recovery

**Cool-down:** 5 minutes of easy riding

**Comments:** This workout simulates a race effort. It will help if you visualize riding up the climb with the peloton at a moderately hard pace and then attacking the final two minutes of the effort and riding as hard as you can to the finish.

## H4:   Hill Training

**Total time:** 45 minutes

**Warm-up:** 10 minutes of easy riding

**Terrain:** Uphill long, steady grade, or on an indoor trainer

**Workout:** 3 × 6 minutes, with 6 minutes of easy spinning downhill between intervals

**Pace:** Steady, hard to very hard

**Training zone during intervals:** 4

> MaxHR for training zone _____
>
> LTHR for training zone _____

**Training zone during recovery:** 1

> MaxHR for training zone _____
>
> LTHR for training zone _____

**Effort:** RPE 8-9 during intervals, RPE 1-2 during recovery

**RPM:** 80-95 during intervals, 100-110 during recovery

**Cool-down:** 5 minutes of easy riding

**Comments:** Focus on maintaining a steady effort during these intervals. Alternate standing and sitting on the climb to maintain your speed, and keep your effort level high throughout.

## H5:  Hill Training

**Total time:** 35 minutes

**Warm-up:** 10 minutes of easy riding

**Terrain:** Uphill long, steady grade, or on an indoor trainer

**Workout:** 20-minute climb, alternating between 2 minutes at a hard pace and 2 minutes at a medium pace for the duration of the climb

**Pace:** Staccato, alternating between hard and medium

**Training zone during first 2 minutes:** 4

MaxHR for training zone _____

LTHR for training zone _____

**Training zone during second 2 minutes:** 2

MaxHR for training zone _____

LTHR for training zone _____

**Effort:** RPE 8-9 during work in zone 4, RPE 3-5 during work in zone 2

**RPM:** 80-100

**Cool-down:** 5 minutes of easy riding

**Comments:** This workout mimics a race effort, where the pace constantly changes as riders race each other up a climb, attacking and then slowing. During this workout, envision yourself in a race. Imagine yourself attacking your competitors and dropping them on the climbs, and toward the end of the interval you are alone heading to victory. This visualization helps to make the interval more exciting, and you will also get more out of yourself physically.

## H6:   Hill Training

**Total time:** 65 minutes

**Warm-up:** 10 minutes of easy riding

**Terrain:** Uphill long,steady grade, or on an indoor trainer

**Workout:** 2 × 20-minute climb, alternating between 2 minutes at a hard pace and 2 minutes at a medium pace for the duration of each climb, with 10 minutes of coasting and easy spinning downhill between climbs

**Pace:** Staccato, alternating between hard and medium

### Training zone during first 2 minutes: 4

MaxHR for training zone _____

LTHR for training zone _____

### Training zone during second 2 minutes: 2

MaxHR for training zone _____

LTHR for training zone _____

### Training zone during recovery: 1

MaxHR for training zone _____

LTHR for training zone _____

**Effort:** RPE 8-9 during work in zone 4, RPE 3-5 during work in zone 2, RPE 1 during recovery

**RPM:** 80-100 during climbs, 100-110 during recovery

**Cool-down:** 5 minutes of easy riding

**Comments:** You will sweat and burn a lot of calories; therefore, to get the most out of your workout, you must sustain your energy levels by drinking fluids between these sets. Eating an energy gel, which is easy to digest, halfway through the workout is also a good idea.

# H7:   Hill Training

**Total time:** 59 minutes

**Warm-up:** 10 minutes of easy riding

**Terrain:** Uphill long, steady grade, or on an indoor trainer

**Workout:** 6 × 4 minutes with 4 minutes of easy spinning downhill between intervals

**Pace:** Steady, very hard

**Training zone during intervals:** 4-5

        MaxHR for training zone _____

        LTHR for training zone _____

**Training zone during recovery:** 1

        MaxHR for training zone _____

        LTHR for training zone _____

**Effort:** RPE 8-10 during intervals, RPE 1 during recovery

**RPM:** 90-100 during intervals, 100-110 during recovery

**Cool-down:** 5 minutes of easy riding

**Comments:** The recovery time is as important as the interval. Four minutes will go by quickly, especially toward the end of the series, so be sure your heart rate slows as much as possible. Breathe deeply and calmly to refill your muscles with oxygen before you get back on the pedals and attack the next interval.

## H8:  Hill Training

**Total time:** 54-72 minutes (will vary based on recovery time)

**Warm-up:** 10 minutes of easy riding

**Terrain:** Uphill steady grade

**Workout:** 7 × 3 minutes with full recovery between intervals (3 to 6 minutes)

**Pace:** Steady, very hard

**Training zone during intervals:** 4-5

> MaxHR for training zone _____
>
> LTHR for training zone _____

**Training zone during recovery:** 1

> MaxHR for training zone _____
>
> LTHR for training zone _____

**Effort:** RPE 8-10 during intervals, RPE 1 during recovery

**RPM:** 90-100 during intervals, 100-110 during recovery

**Cool-down:** 5 minutes of easy riding

**Comments:** These are difficult intervals and require a lot of effort, but they are over quickly. You'll feel tired afterward, but there is nothing like cruising home after a successful interval session knowing you have put in a solid effort and that you're getting stronger.

## H9:   Hill Training

**Total time:** Approximately 36 minutes

**Warm-up:** 10 minutes of easy riding

**Terrain:** Uphill long, steady grade

**Workout:** 10 × 20 seconds with 2 minutes of recovery between intervals (still continuing uphill)

**Pace:** Staccato, alternating between very hard and medium

**Training zone during intervals:** 5

        MaxHR for training zone _____

        LTHR for training zone _____

**Training zone during recovery:** 2

        MaxHR for training zone _____

        LTHR for training zone _____

**Effort:** RPE 10 during intervals, RPE 3-5 during recovery

**RPM:** 90-100 during intervals, 100-110 during recovery

**Cool-down:** 5 minutes of easy riding

**Comments:** Attack the zone 5 efforts as hard as possible—like you are racing away from the peloton. Then ease up a little and recover, but don't go too easy, and then attack again. Imagine you're in the race: You attack, get caught, ride in the peloton, attack again, get caught by fewer riders, and then repeat the attack. These are great race simulation intervals that work your body as well as your mind.

## H10:  Hill Training

**Total time:** Approximately 40 minutes

**Warm-up:** 10 minutes of easy riding

**Terrain:** Uphill steady grade

**Workout:** 4 × 1 kilometer (0.6 miles) with full recovery between intervals

**Pace:** Steady, very hard

**Training zone during intervals:** 5

>  MaxHR for training zone _____

>  LTHR for training zone _____

**Training zone during recovery:** 1

>  MaxHR for training zone _____

>  LTHR for training zone _____

**Effort:** RPE 9-10 during intervals, RPE 1 during recovery

**RPM:** 90-100 during intervals, 100-110 during recovery

**Cool-down:** 5 minutes of easy riding

**Comments:** Get up to speed by standing up out of the saddle, and then settle back into the saddle, going as hard as you can. Treat each effort like it is a race. Go as hard as you can for one kilometer (0.6 miles).

# H11:  Hill Training

**Total time:** Approximately 50 minutes

**Warm-up:** 10 minutes of easy riding

**Terrain:** Uphill steady grade

**Workout:** 7 × 1 kilometer (0.6 miles) with full recovery between intervals

**Pace:** Steady, very hard

**Training zone during intervals:** 5

> MaxHR for training zone _____
>
> LTHR for training zone _____

**Training zone during recovery:** 1

> MaxHR for training zone _____
>
> LTHR for training zone _____

**Effort:** RPE 10 during intervals, RPE 1 during recovery

**RPM:** 90-100 during intervals, 100-110 during recovery

**Cool-down:** 5 minutes of easy riding

**Comments:** These types of efforts are similar to the kind of effort you must make when attacking on a hill in a race. As you complete these intervals, visualize yourself attacking, breaking away from the peloton, and winning a race and you will gain a few watts of power.

## H12:  Hill Training

**Total time:** Approximately 55 minutes

**Warm-up:** 10 minutes of easy riding

**Terrain:** Uphill steady grade

**Workout:** 7 × 120 seconds, the first 90 seconds beginning at an easy pace and increasing to all-out for the final 30 seconds, with full recovery between intervals

**Pace:** Increasing from easy to all-out

### Training zone during first 90 seconds: 2

MaxHR for training zone _____

LTHR for training zone _____

### Training zone during final 30 seconds: 5

MaxHR for training zone _____

LTHR for training zone _____

### Training zone during recovery: 1

MaxHR for training zone _____

LTHR for training zone _____

**Effort:** RPE 3-5 during work in zone 2, RPE 10 during work in zone 5, RPE 1 during recovery

**RPM:** 90-100 during intervals, 100-110 during recovery

**Cool-down:** 5 minutes of easy riding

**Comments:** Attack the 30-second efforts in zone 5 like you are attacking in a race. Get out of the saddle and go as fast as you can. If this does not create a burning sensation in your legs, you are not going hard enough. This workout simulates a maximal race effort.

CHAPTER **9**

# Time Trial Workouts

Time trial training will help you to maximize your steady-state speed on flat to rolling terrain and prepare you for time trial race efforts, or races against the clock. If you are not interested in racing or time-trialing, these workouts may not seem important to you, but time trial training benefits riders of all levels. Fitness cyclists, cycling enthusiasts, and racers who don't race time trial events will increase their steady-state speed on flat to rolling terrain by doing this type of training and will begin to ride faster and more efficiently.

You will be ready for the training in this chapter after having completed three to four weeks of strength and lactate threshold training. Like the hill-training workouts, these workouts should be done at a hard or very hard intensity on flat to hilly terrain or indoors on a home trainer or ergometer. The interval workouts in this chapter are listed from long, hard efforts to shorter, very hard efforts with race simulation at the end, helping you build toward your fitness, race, or event peak.

The time trial is the purest form of bike racing because it is simply the rider against the clock. It was Dede's favorite event, and she focused much of her training to become a specialist in the discipline. Her hard work paid off when she won the silver medal in the women's individual time trial at the 2004 Olympic Games.

The workouts begin with 10-minute time trial intervals. The first three workouts have the same interval lengths, but build up in repetitions. Beginning and intermediate riders should begin with workout 1 and build up. Workout 3 is challenging and may be too much for a beginning rider. As the workouts progress, the intervals shorten, but become more intense, as the amount of riding in zone 5 increases. Most of the workouts are meant for riders of all levels, but we advise that workout 7 will be challenging for beginning riders and workout 10 is extremely difficult and is meant only for advanced riders. The final two workouts are time trial tests. Beginning riders should test themselves on the shorter course in workout 11; intermediate and advanced riders can choose or test themselves on both types of courses. Table 9.1 lists the workout times and interval intensity levels for the various time trial workouts detailed in this chapter.

### Table 9.1  Preview: Time Trial Workouts

| Workout | Total workout time (min) | Intensity (HR zone/RPE) |
|---------|--------------------------|-------------------------|
| TT1 | 45 | 4/8-9 |
| TT2 | 65 | 4/8-9 |
| TT3 | 85 | 4/8-9 |
| TT4 | 55 | 4/8-9 |
| TT5 | 57 | 4/8-9 |
| TT6 | 50 | 4-5/8-10 |
| TT7 | 70 | 4-5/8-10 |
| TT8 | 59 | 4-5/8-10 |
| TT9 | 58 | 4-5/8-10 |
| TT10 | 113 | 4-5/8-10 |
| TT11 | approx. 35-50 | 4-5/8-10 |
| TT12 | approx. 50-65 | 4-5/8-10 |

# TT1: Time Trial Training

**Total time:** 45 minutes

**Warm-up:** 10 minutes of easy riding

**Terrain:** Flat to rolling, without stoplights or stop signs, or on an indoor trainer

**Workout:** 2 × 10 minutes with 10 minutes of recovery between intervals

**Pace:** Steady, very hard

**Training zone during intervals:** 4

        MaxHR for training zone _____

        LTHR for training zone _____

**Training zone during recovery:** 1

        MaxHR for training zone _____

        LTHR for training zone _____

**Effort:** RPE 8-9 during intervals, RPE 1 during recovery

**RPM:** 80-95 during intervals, 100-110 during recovery

**Cool-down:** 5 minutes of easy riding

**Comments:** When you are time-trialing, pacing is important: You must ride at a pace that you can sustain for the total distance. While doing this workout, keep your speed steady by looking at your bike computer periodically and making adjustments as needed.

## TT2: Time Trial Training

**Total time:** 65 minutes

**Warm-up:** 10 minutes of easy riding

**Terrain:** Flat to rolling, without stoplights or stop signs, or on an indoor trainer

**Workout:** 3 × 10 minutes with 10 minutes of recovery between intervals

**Pace:** Steady, very hard

**Training zone during intervals:** 4

        MaxHR for training zone _____

        LTHR for training zone _____

**Training zone during recovery:** 1

        MaxHR for training zone _____

        LTHR for training zone _____

**Effort:** RPE 8-9 during intervals, RPE 1 during recovery

**RPM:** 80-95 during intervals, 100-110 during recovery

**Cool-down:** 5 minutes of easy riding

**Comments:** Focus on pedaling smooth circles and keeping a relaxed body, especially as you begin to fatigue. Pull up and push down on the pedals evenly. Thinking about your pedaling technique will help distract you from the pain, push harder, and go faster.

# TT3:   Time Trial Training

**Total time:** 85 minutes

**Warm-up:** 10 minutes of easy riding

**Terrain:** Flat to rolling, without stoplights or stop signs, or on an indoor trainer

**Workout:** 4 × 10 minutes with 10 minutes of recovery between intervals

**Pace:** Steady, very hard

**Training zone during intervals:** 4

> MaxHR for training zone _____

> LTHR for training zone _____

**Training zone during recovery:** 1

> MaxHR for training zone _____

> LTHR for training zone _____

**Effort:** RPE 8-9 during intervals, RPE 1 during recovery

**RPM:** 80-95 during intervals, 100-110 during recovery

**Cool-down:** 5 minutes of easy riding

**Comments:** This workout is long and intense, so be sure to drink enough fluids and perhaps eat an energy bar or gel between the intervals. This will help you to finish the workout strongly. Try to find the most aerodynamic position, and focus on keeping relaxed in this position. You want to be aerodynamic, but at the same time you want to be able to produce the power to go fast. Find what works for your body type; some riders are flexible and can tuck themselves way down on their bikes, whereas others lose all their power if they are too low.

## TT4:   Time Trial Training

**Total time:** 55 minutes

**Warm-up:** 10 minutes of easy riding

**Terrain:** Flat to rolling, without stoplights or stop signs, or on an indoor trainer

**Workout:** 3 × 8 minutes with 8 minutes of recovery between intervals

**Pace:** Steady, very hard

**Training zone during intervals:** 4

       MaxHR for training zone _____

       LTHR for training zone _____

**Training zone during recovery:** 1

       MaxHR for training zone _____

       LTHR for training zone _____

**Effort:** RPE 8-9 during intervals, RPE 1 during recovery

**RPM:** 90-110 during intervals, 100-110 during recovery

**Cool-down:** 5 minutes of easy riding

**Comments:** Focus on your breathing during the time trial efforts. You don't want to gasp or pant, but you do want a rhythmic breathing pattern. Time-trialing well is all about breathing, concentrating, and remaining aerodynamic.

# TT5:   Time Trial Training

**Total time:** 57 minutes

**Warm-up:** 10 minutes of easy riding

**Terrain:** Flat to rolling, without stoplights or stop signs, or on an indoor trainer

**Workout:** 4 × 6 minutes with 6 minutes of recovery between intervals

**Pace:** Steady, very hard

**Training zone during intervals:** 4

>       MaxHR for training zone _____

>       LTHR for training zone _____

**Training zone during recovery:** 1

>       MaxHR for training zone _____

>       LTHR for training zone _____

**Effort:** RPE 8-9 during intervals, RPE 1 during recovery

**RPM:** 90-110 during intervals, 100-110 during recovery

**Cool-down:** 5 minutes of easy riding

**Comments:** When you start your interval, don't sprint to get up to speed. Instead, progressively increase the effort over about 500 meters (0.3 miles) to keep from producing lactic acid. Start in a fairly easy, or low, gear and work your way down through the gears.

# TT6:   Time Trial Training

**Total time:** 50 minutes

**Warm-up:** 10 minutes of easy riding

**Terrain:** Flat to rolling, without stoplights or stop signs, or on an indoor trainer

**Workout:** 4 × 5 minutes with 5 minutes of recovery between intervals

**Pace:** Steady, very hard

**Training zone during intervals:** 4-5

> MaxHR for training zone _____
>
> LTHR for training zone _____

**Training zone during recovery:** 1

> MaxHR for training zone _____
>
> LTHR for training zone _____

**Effort:** RPE 8-10 during intervals, RPE 1 during recovery

**RPM:** 90-110 during intervals, 100-110 during recovery

**Cool-down:** 5 minutes of easy riding

**Comments:** During the intervals, focus on the road ahead of you: Pick a point in the distance, focus your eyes on it, and then keep your upper body still while your legs pump away. Concentrate at all times, and ask yourself, "Am I pedaling the best I can? Am I pedaling in circles? Am I aerodynamic?" Don't let your mind drift and start thinking about the movie you're going to watch that night or the big burrito you're going to eat after your workout. These thoughts will slow you down; keep your mind on your goal.

# TT7:   Time Trial Training

**Total time:** 70 minutes

**Warm-up:** 10 minutes of easy riding

**Terrain:** Flat to rolling, without stoplights or stop signs, or on an indoor trainer

**Workout:** 6 × 5 minutes with 5 minutes of recovery between intervals

**Pace:** Steady, very hard

**Training zone during intervals:** 4-5

       MaxHR for training zone _____

       LTHR for training zone _____

**Training zone during recovery:** 1

       MaxHR for training zone _____

       LTHR for training zone _____

**Effort:** RPE 8-10 during intervals, RPE 1 during recovery

**RPM:** 90-110 during intervals, 100-110 during recovery

**Cool-down:** 5 minutes of easy riding

**Comments:** Before the Olympics in Athens, Dede did many intervals just like these, and they were a big reason why she was able to win a silver medal. Practicing the discipline will make you mentally and physically stronger.

# TT8: Time Trial Training

**Total time:** 59 minutes

**Warm-up:** 10 minutes of easy riding

**Terrain:** Flat to rolling, without stoplights or stop signs, or on an indoor trainer

**Workout:** 6 × 4 minutes with 4 minutes of recovery between intervals

**Pace:** Steady, very hard

**Training zone during intervals:** 4-5

> MaxHR for training zone _____
>
> LTHR for training zone _____

**Training zone during recovery:** 1

> MaxHR for training zone _____
>
> LTHR for training zone _____

**Effort:** RPE 8-10 during intervals, RPE 1 during recovery

**RPM:** 90-110 during intervals, 100-110 during recovery

**Cool-down:** 5 minutes of easy riding

**Comments:** When you're recovering from the time trial intervals, spin your legs out in a light gear, making sure you're not putting pressure on them but that you're clearing out the aches, pains, and lactic acid from your last effort.

# TT9:   Time Trial Training

**Total time:** 58 minutes

**Warm-up:** 10 minutes of easy riding

**Terrain:** Flat to rolling, without stoplights or stop signs, or on an indoor trainer

**Workout:** 6 × 3 minutes with 5 minutes of recovery between intervals

**Pace:** Steady, very hard

**Training zone during intervals:** 4-5

      MaxHR for training zone _____

      LTHR for training zone _____

**Training zone during recovery:** 1

      MaxHR for training zone _____

      LTHR for training zone _____

**Effort:** RPE 8-10 during intervals, RPE 1 during recovery

**RPM:** 90-110 during intervals, 100-110 during recovery

**Cool-down:** 5 minutes of easy riding

**Comments:** Get up to speed before you start the clock on these intervals. Try to race yourself by tracking your average speed. Try to beat your average speed records each time you do this workout.

# TT10: Time Trial Training

**Total time:** 113 minutes

**Warm-up:** 10 minutes of easy riding

**Terrain:** Flat to rolling, without stoplights or stop signs, or on an indoor trainer

**Workout:** 2 minutes, 4 minutes, 6 minutes, 8 minutes, 10 minutes, 8 minutes, 6 minutes, 4 minutes, and 2 minutes with recovery time between each interval equal to the interval just completed

**Pace:** Steady, very hard

**Training zone during intervals:** 4-5

        MaxHR for training zone _____

        LTHR for training zone _____

**Training zone during recovery:** 1

        MaxHR for training zone _____

        LTHR for training zone _____

**Effort:** RPE 8-10 during intervals, RPE 1 during recovery

**RPM:** 90-110 during intervals, 100-110 during recovery

**Cool-down:** 5 minutes of easy riding

**Comments:** Pyramid intervals like these help you to maximize your top-end speed. Go all out on each interval. Your average speed will be higher on the shorter intervals and a little lower on the longer intervals.

# TT11: Time Trial Test

**Total time:** Approximately 35-50 minutes

**Warm-up:** 10 minutes of easy riding

**Terrain:** Flat to rolling, without stoplights or stop signs, or on an indoor trainer

**Workout:** 10-kilometer (6-mile) time trial

**Pace:** Steady, very hard, all out

**Training zone:** 4-5

MaxHR for training zone _____

LTHR for training zone _____

**Effort:** RPE 8-10

**RPM:** 85-110

**Cool-down:** 5 minutes of easy riding

**Comments:** Treat this test like a race and motivate yourself to go all out! This time trial will test your fitness level. Log all information pertaining to this effort: average speed, watts, distance, weather conditions, and RPE. This information will be valuable when comparing future test data, because it will allow you to gauge your fitness improvements.

## TT12: Time Trial Test

**Total time:** Approximately 50-65 minutes

**Warm-up:** 10 minutes of easy riding

**Terrain:** Flat to rolling, without stoplights or stop signs, or on an indoor trainer

**Workout:** 20-kilometer (12-mile) time trial

**Pace:** Steady, very hard, all out

**Training zone:** 4-5

       MaxHR for training zone _____

       LTHR for training zone _____

**Effort:** RPE 8-10

**RPM:** 85-110

**Cool-down:** 5 minutes of easy riding

**Comments:** Focus on pacing. Go at a speed that you can maintain for approximately 30 minutes. You do not want to start out too fast and die, and likewise, you want to reach your maximum effort so that you get an accurate test of your fitness level. Log all information pertaining to this effort: average speed, watts, distance, weather conditions, and RPE. This information will be valuable when comparing future test data because it will allow you to gauge your fitness improvements.

# 10

# Speed Workouts

After three to four weeks of hill training or time trial training, you will be ready for speedwork. The time trial workouts in the last chapter were done mainly in zone 4 with some zone 5 intensity, but as you advance to the speedwork intervals, the majority of the intervals will be done in zone 5. The intervals will generally be much shorter than the time trial intervals as well, with most of the intervals being 20 seconds to 2 minutes in length. While the time trial workouts helped you to achieve maximal steady-state speed with anaerobic bursts at the end, the speed-work intervals will help you to improve your anaerobic and maximal sprinting speed.

The workouts in this chapter require maximal effort and prepare you for a specific race or for peak fitness. Speed workouts with proper recovery are necessary for attaining optimal fitness. The workouts are full of short, intense efforts and race simulations. The high intensity puts a heavy load on your legs; therefore, you must give your body more recovery time between workouts. The workouts are listed from hardest to easiest. This is because in previous training you have progressively built toward maximum intensity in order to stimulate all your energy systems. Once you reach this maximal level, you must reduce the total amount of work in your training, allowing your body to adapt and obtain optimal fitness. The final workouts in this chapter simulate specific races and provide great preparation 3 to 10 days before a race or peak event.

The workouts begin with longer intervals of up to 5 minutes and then shorten to 20 seconds, with race simulation in the final workouts. The first workout is a pyramid interval workout that is meant for all levels of cyclists. The number of intervals in workout 2 may be a little challenging for beginner cyclists, but a beginning cyclist should do as many of the intervals as possible. Workout 3 is extremely challenging and is meant for advanced cyclists. Workout 4 is a shorter version of workout 3 and is for beginning to intermediate riders. Workouts 5, 6, and 7 are short and intense intervals. They are meant for all levels, but two sets are included in the workouts and only one set is necessary for a beginning rider. Workouts 8 and 9 are not as intense as the other workouts in this chapter; however, they are still to be performed by all levels of cyclists because these workouts involve pedaling at a high rate of RPM, which helps ready the leg muscles for a race or event. As such, workouts 8 and 9 should be performed during the week leading up to a race or peak event. Workout 10 is a sprint workout that is primarily meant for racers, but all levels of cyclists can enjoy winding their bike up to full speed. Training your sprint will prepare you for the final meters of a bike race when you need to rush to the line as quickly as possible in an attempt to win or place. Workouts 11 and 12 are race simulations meant to simulate the type of effort you would exert in a road race or criterium. These two workouts can benefit all levels of cyclists because they provide the opportunity to improve bike-handling skills while pushing the rider to his or her maximum potential. Table 10.1 lists the workout times and interval intensity levels for the various speed workouts detailed in this chapter.

## Table 10.1 Preview: Speed Workouts

| Workout | Total workout time (min) | Intensity (HR zone/RPE) |
|---------|--------------------------|--------------------------|
| S1 | 64 | 4-5/9-10 |
| S2 | approx. 65 | 3/6-7 and 5/10 |
| S3 | 44 | 5/10 |
| S4 | 34 | 5/10 |
| S5 | approx. 45 | 5/10 |
| S6 | approx. 45 | 5/10 |
| S7 | approx. 30-40 | 5/10 |
| S8 | 55 | 1-2/2-5 and 3-4/3-9 |
| S9 | 45 | 3-4/6-9 |
| S10 | approx. 60 | 3-4/6-9 and 5/10 |
| S11 | approx. 65 | 4/8-9 and 5/10 |
| S12 | approx. 50-65 | 4/8-9 and 5/10 |

# S1:    Speed Training

**Total time:** 64 minutes

**Warm-up:** 10 minutes of easy riding

**Terrain:** Flat to rolling landscape, or on an indoor trainer

**Workout:** 1 minute, 2 minutes, 3 minutes, 4 minutes, 5 minutes, 4 minutes, 3 minutes, 2 minutes, and 1 minute with recovery time between each interval equal to the interval just completed

**Pace:** Very fast

**Training zone during intervals:** 4-5

> MaxHR for training zone _____
>
> LTHR for training zone _____

**Training zone during recovery:** 1

> MaxHR for training zone _____
>
> LTHR for training zone _____

**Effort:** RPE 9-10 during intervals, RPE 1 during recovery

**RPM:** 90-110 during intervals, 100-110 during recovery

**Cool-down:** 5 minutes of easy riding

**Comments:** This pyramid workout is an intense leg and lung burner. Attack the shorter one- and two-minute intervals like you are attacking in a race. Maintain steady effort levels and speed during the three-, four-, and five-minute intervals.

## S2:    Speed Training

**Total time:** Approximately 65 minutes

**Warm-up:** 10 minutes of easy riding

**Terrain:** Flat to rolling landscape, or on an indoor trainer

**Workout:** 10 × 90 seconds, each interval consisting of 60 seconds at a hard pace and 30 seconds all-out, with full recovery between intervals

**Pace:** Very fast

**Training zone during first 60 seconds of interval:** 3

> MaxHR for training zone _____
>
> LTHR for training zone _____

**Training zone during second 30 seconds of interval:** 5

> MaxHR for training zone _____
>
> LTHR for training zone _____

**Training zone during recovery:** 1

> MaxHR for training zone _____
>
> LTHR for training zone _____

**Effort:** RPE 6-7 during work in zone 3, RPE 10 during work in zone 5, RPE 1 during recovery

**RPM:** 90-115

**Cool-down:** 5 minutes of easy riding

**Comments:** These intervals are similar to a solo effort off the front of the peloton with only a couple kilometers to go in the race. Focus on making the last 30 seconds count. Imagine that you are going to win the biggest race of your life, and your competitors are charging toward you from behind. You must pedal as fast and as hard as possible to win the race.

# S3:    Speed Training

**Total time:** 44 minutes

**Warm-up:** 10 minutes of easy riding

**Terrain:** Flat, without stoplights or stop signs, or on an indoor trainer

**Workout:** 15 × 1 minute with 1 minute of recovery between intervals

**Pace:** Very fast

**Training zone during intervals:** 5

> MaxHR for training zone _____

> LTHR for training zone _____

**Training zone during recovery:** 1

> MaxHR for training zone _____

> LTHR for training zone _____

**Effort:** RPE 10 during intervals, RPE 1 during recovery

**RPM:** 90-115 during intervals, 100-110 during recovery

**Cool-down:** 5 minutes of easy riding

**Comments:** This workout is extremely intense. You must go all out and then recover and because the recovery is not very long, you end up with a very high average heart rate. You must maintain an average of 100 RPM throughout this workout. This means you will shift gears every minute to maintain the proper intensity and RPM level. This workout requires intense concentration. At the end, if you have done the workout correctly, you will feel fatigue and lactic acid in your legs.

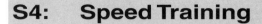

# S4:    Speed Training

**Total time:** 34 minutes

**Warm-up:** 10 minutes of easy riding

**Terrain:** Flat, without stoplights or stop signs, or on an indoor trainer

**Workout:** 10 × 1 minute with 1 minute of recovery between intervals

**Pace:** Very fast

**Training zone during intervals:** 5

> MaxHR for training zone _____
>
> LTHR for training zone _____

**Training zone during recovery:** 1

> MaxHR for training zone _____
>
> LTHR for training zone _____

**Effort:** RPE 10 during intervals, RPE 1-2 during recovery

**RPM:** 90-115 during intervals, 100-110 during recovery

**Cool-down:** 5 minutes of easy riding

**Comments:** There is no question that this workout is difficult, and it becomes progressively more difficult toward the end. Focus on your pedal stroke. Make it is as powerful and fluid as possible. Pull up hard on your pedals on the upstroke and push hard on the downstroke. This is a workout that everyone finds tough, but one that is essential for improving overall high-end fitness.

# S5:   Speed Training

**Total time:** Approximately 45 minutes

**Warm-up:** 10 minutes of easy riding

**Terrain:** Flat, without stoplights or stop signs

**Workout:** 2 sets of 1 × 30 seconds, 60 seconds, 90 seconds, 60 seconds, and 30 seconds with recovery time between each interval equal to the interval just completed; 5-15 minute full recovery between sets

**Pace:** Very fast

**Training zone during intervals:** 5

> MaxHR for training zone _____
>
> LTHR for training zone _____

**Training zone during recovery:** 1

> MaxHR for training zone _____
>
> LTHR for training zone _____

**Effort:** RPE 10 during intervals, RPE 1-2 during recovery

**RPM:** 90-115 during intervals, 100-110 during recovery

**Cool-down:** 5 minutes of easy riding

**Comments:** This pyramid workout will seem tough at first, but it will fly by. These efforts will cause discomfort in your legs and lungs, but the intervals are short, so try to push through the pain to build your engine and become a stronger cyclist.

## S6: Speed Training

**Total time:** Approximately 45 minutes

**Warm-up:** 10 minutes of easy riding

**Terrain:** Flat, without stoplights or stop signs

**Workout:** 2 sets of 5 × 30 seconds with 90 seconds of recovery between intervals; 10-15 minute full recovery between sets

**Pace:** Very fast

**Training zone during intervals:** 5

  MaxHR for training zone _____

  LTHR for training zone _____

**Training zone during recovery:** 1

  MaxHR for training zone _____

  LTHR for training zone _____

**Effort:** RPE 10 during intervals, RPE 1-2 during recovery

**RPM:** 90-115 during intervals, 100-110 during recovery

**Cool-down:** 5 minutes of easy riding

**Comments:** These sprints will build your top-end power. Start as hard as possible and sustain it for 30 seconds. As you tire toward the end, keep pushing with every ounce of energy you have left. These intervals are short but sweet; they hurt, but they will make you faster in a sprint.

# S7:    Speed Training

**Total time:** Approximately 30-40 minutes

**Warm-up:** 10 minutes of easy riding

**Terrain:** Flat, without stoplights or stop signs

**Workout:** 2 sets of 5 × 15 seconds with 45 seconds of recovery between intervals; 10-15 minute full recovery between sets

**Pace:** Very fast

**Training zone during intervals:** 5

       MaxHR for training zone _____

       LTHR for training zone _____

**Training zone during recovery:** 1

       MaxHR for training zone _____

       LTHR for training zone _____

**Effort:** RPE 10 during intervals, RPE 1 during recovery

**RPM:** 90-115 during intervals, 100-110 during recovery

**Cool-down:** 5 minutes of easy riding

**Comments:** Focus on getting up to speed as quickly as possible. Not only will this work your lungs, but your arm and leg muscles will also feel the burn as you push and pull to get the bike up to speed and flying.

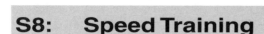
## S8:   Speed Training

**Total time:** 55 minutes

**Warm-up:** 10 minutes of easy riding

**Terrain:** Flat, without stoplights or stop signs, or on an indoor trainer

**Workout:** 1 × 45 minutes, increasing RPM every 5 minutes

**Pace:** Steady, medium to very fast

**Training zone during start of interval:** 1-2

> MaxHR for training zone _____

> LTHR for training zone _____

**Training zone during peak effort:** 3-4

> MaxHR for training zone _____

> LTHR for training zone _____

**Effort:** RPE 2-5 during work in zones 1-2, RPE 3-9 during work in zones 3-4

**RPM:** 5 minutes at 80 RPM, 5 minutes at 85 RPM, 5 minutes at 90 RPM, 5 minutes at 95 RPM, 5 minutes at 100 RPM, 5 minutes at 105 RPM, 5 minutes at 110 RPM, 5 minutes at 115 RPM

**Cool-down:** 5 minutes of easy riding

**Comments:** This workout works on leg speed, lactate threshold, and endurance. Because you are forced to ride at high RPM, this workout makes your legs more fluid and snappier. This is great preparation two or three days before a big race. Be sure to use the same gear throughout the workout.

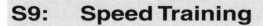

# S9:    Speed Training

**Total time:** 45 minutes

**Warm-up:** 10 minutes of easy riding

**Terrain:** Flat to rolling, or on an indoor trainer

**Workout:** 30-minute ride at high RPM

**Pace:** Medium to fast (if done on rolling terrain, heart rate and effort levels will increase on the ascents and decrease on the descents, creating a gentle interval effect)

**Training zone:** 3-4

MaxHR for training zone _____

LTHR for training zone _____

**Effort:** RPE 6-9

**RPM:** 100-120

**Cool-down:** 5 minutes of easy riding

**Comments:** Riding at high RPM will make your legs supple and speedy. This is great preparation in the final days before a race. Try not to bob up and down when you are spinning your legs. Keep the motion in your legs and not in your back and hips. The upper body should be perfectly still while your legs pump away like pistons.

## S10:   Speed Training

**Total time:** Approximately 60 minutes

**Warm-up:** 10 minutes of easy riding

**Terrain:** Flat to rolling

**Workout:** 6 × 200-meter sprints; steadily build up speed for 1 kilometer (0.6 miles), then all-out sprint for 200 meters; 5-15 minute full recovery between intervals

**Pace:** Very fast

**Training zone during 1-kilometer lead-up:** 3-4

MaxHR for training zone _____

LTHR for training zone _____

**Training zone during 200-meter sprint:** 5

MaxHR for training zone _____

LTHR for training zone _____

**Training zone during recovery:** 1

MaxHR for training zone _____

LTHR for training zone _____

**Effort:** RPE 6-9 during work in zones 3-4, RPE 10 during work in zone 5, RPE 1 during recovery

**RPM:** 90-115 during lead-up and sprints, 100-110 during recovery

**Cool-down:** 5 minutes of easy riding

**Comments:** Do this workout with at least one other person if possible. You will push yourself harder when competing with someone else. You can take turns leading the 1,000-meter lead-up and then race each other in the final 200 meters. Michael and his teammates often sprint each other during their training rides to sharpen their skills and prepare themselves for races. Pick a town sign or marker on the roadside and make that your finish line. The rider who wins the most sprints buys the drinks after the workout!

# S11:  Speed Training: Race Simulation

**Total time:** Approximately 65 minutes

**Warm-up:** 10 minutes of easy riding

**Terrain:** Flat to rolling

**Workout:** 1 × 10-minute time trial with 10-minute recovery, then 4 × 1 kilometer (0.6 miles) with 3-minute recovery between intervals

**Pace:** Very fast (get up to speed as quickly as possible and maintain it)

**Training zone during 10-minute time trial:** 4

   MaxHR for training zone _____

   LTHR for training zone _____

**Training zone during 1-kilometer intervals:** 5

   MaxHR for training zone _____

   LTHR for training zone _____

**Training zone during each recovery:** 1

   MaxHR for training zone _____

   LTHR for training zone _____

**Effort:** RPE 8-9 during time trial, RPE 10 during 1-kilometer intervals, RPE 1 during each recovery

**RPM:** 90-110

**Cool-down:** 5 minutes of easy riding

**Comments:** This workout will build your overall high end. Schedule it as a big event is nearing because it not only prepares you for the longer efforts in a race but also the shorter repetitions that you might do toward the end of the race.

# S12: Speed Training: Race Simulation

**Total time:** Approximately 50-65 minutes

**Warm-up:** 10 minutes of easy riding

**Terrain:** Flat to rolling

**Workout:** 20 minutes at a steady, hard pace followed by intervals of 3 minutes, 2 minutes, 1 minute, and 30 seconds at an all-out pace, with recovery time between the all-out intervals equal (at least) to the interval just completed

**Pace:** Steady, fast pace for the 20-minute ride; very fast, all-out pace for other intervals

**Training zone during the 20-minute interval:** 4

> MaxHR for training zone _____
>
> LTHR for training zone _____

**Training zone during all other intervals:** 5

> MaxHR for training zone _____
>
> LTHR for training zone _____

**Training zone during recovery:** 1

> MaxHR for training zone _____
>
> LTHR for training zone _____

**Effort:** RPE 8-9 during work in zone 4, RPE 10 during work in zone 5, RPE 1 during recovery

**RPM:** 90-115 during all intervals, 100-110 during recovery

**Cool-down:** 5 minutes of easy riding

**Comments:** Be sure to pace yourself over the first segment of the workout so that you have energy left to give in the last intervals. This is a tough workout, so make sure you are fully recovered between intervals. If you need more rest, take it—the key is to be able to ride at the right intensity while doing the intervals. You should be proud of your accomplishment after completing this workout!

# Part III

# The Programs

Cyclists have different definitions of fitness. Some consider fitness the ability to exercise enough to provide health benefits. Others see fitness as a marker of how fast they can ride their bikes. Professional cyclists view fitness as the key to their livelihood. All types of cyclists will benefit from improving their fitness, and the training programs outlined in this book will profoundly improve your fitness. Following a training program will help you to look at the big picture and maintain your focus and motivation as you work toward your peak. We have laid out periodized training programs for the beginner, intermediate, and advanced cyclists with individual workouts that fit into an overall plan to give you the most benefit for time you spend training. Each of the first four chapters in part III covers one training phase. These phases build on each other to create the overall periodization plan that will help you attain your fitness peak.

Chapter 11 contains a base-building program. It is essential that you build a solid endurance foundation before starting more intense training. The workouts in chapter 12 improve your lactate threshold and strength, which will help you improve your ability to clear lactic acid and increase your steady-state speed for hard efforts of 30 minutes and more. Workouts in chapter 13 help you improve your anaerobic system and build toward peak fitness, preparing you for race-pace efforts of 3 to 10 minutes. Chapter 14 contains speed workouts to help you maintain your fitness and peak for a race or event. Chapter 15 contains cross training ideas and information, which will help you to maintain year-round fitness by participating in other sports in the off-season. It also includes exercises for strengthening your core, which will improve your pedal stroke and prevent injuries and fatigue.

In chapters 11 through 14, you will find three sample programs: beginner, intermediate, and advanced. The workouts in these programs correspond to the workout names and symbols described in part II. The beginner program is much less vigorous and time consuming than the intermediate and advanced programs. A cyclist with little or no riding experience or a cyclist who has a maximum of one hour per day to ride can use the beginner program. The intermediate program is slightly more time consuming and more intense. The advanced program is geared toward more experienced cyclists or endurance athletes who want to push themselves hard and prepare for a challenging race. You must consider several factors when choosing whether to follow the beginner, intermediate, or advanced program:

1.   How much time do you have to train? All three programs suit the rider who, on average, has an hour to work out. But, the workouts in the beginner program total a maximum of one hour, while the intermediate program includes rides up to two hours, and the advanced program contains rides up to three hours.

2.   How much experience do you have in cycling or endurance sports? If you have never ridden a bike consistently or regularly taken part in another endurance sport, you may want to start out with the beginner program. But if you think you can handle riding greater distances than that program has to offer, try the intermediate program. If you have engaged in serious cycling or other endurance sports and are motivated, you can probably handle the advanced program.

Each phase builds on the next, so as you progress through the phases, stick to the program level that you chose at the outset of your training program. And remember to have fun with your training, because that will make you a better, faster cyclist.

# CHAPTER 11

# Building a Base

Every training program should begin with a period of base training. During this 4- to 12-week beginning phase of your training program, you build a solid aerobic foundation. Just as a house needs a strong foundation, so does proper training. It is what everything else stands on. Think of the Egyptian pyramids and their sheer size. If the bottom level, the foundation, was not solid and immense, the peak of the pyramid could never reach the sky. Your aerobic base will do the same for your maximal fitness and will carry you through the entire cycling season.

The riding in this phase is done mainly in zone 2. You will ride at an easy to moderate pace, gradually allowing your body to adjust to riding longer distances and for longer periods of time. Your physiology will change and your muscles will increase their aerobic capacity. The base-building program will vary based on whether you are following the beginner, intermediate, or advanced program. The more base-building workouts you complete, the more solid your foundation will be, so it is best to maximize this phase. Whether you do four, six, eight, or twelve weeks of base training depends on how much training time you have, the point in the year in which you begin your training program, and how many weeks or months you start your training program before your goal event. We recommend a minimum of four weeks of base building before moving on to the lactate threshold and strength building phase. If you want to maximize your base-building phase, but the weather where you live is foul in the winter months, you can substitute aerobic cross training workouts for some of your riding in this phase.

The programs in this chapter consist of four-week blocks so you can choose the amount of base building that works with your schedule. Extending your base-building program to eight or twelve weeks will build a more solid endurance base, which will help you achieve better fitness and maintain it over a longer period of time. When extending your program, follow a pattern of training and recovery days similar to the first four weeks and continue to increase your total time on the bike in each training day. You can follow the program extensions provided or use them as a guide to create your own by adding workouts to the program template in the appendix (page 183). Ultimately, by extending your base-building rides, you will raise your total mileage, increasing your miles in the bank, which will advance your strength, endurance, and fitness as a cyclist.

# BEGINNER PROGRAM

The beginner program is designed for cyclists who are new to the sport or cyclists who have on average one hour or less to work out each day. These rides should feel relatively easy, but some of the longer rides may fatigue you. Over the course of this phase, your endurance will improve, and you will feel more comfortable on the bike. Workouts in the endurance phase should be ridden at a relatively low intensity. Avoid the temptation to ride faster than you are supposed to. You will have plenty of opportunity to increase the intensity in the next phases. You will build up to rides of 90 minutes and become more comfortable on your bike as you increase your time on the bike.

|  | M | Tu | W | Th | F | Sa | Su |
|---|---|---|---|---|---|---|---|
| **Week 1** | Off | E1 | E2 | Off | E1 | E2 | E3 |
| **Week 2** | Off | E2 | E3 | Off | E2 | E3 | E4 |
| **Week 3** | Off | E3 | E4 | Off | E3 | E4 | E5 |
| **Week 4** | Off | E4 | E5 | Off | E4 | E5 | E6 |

|        | M   | Tu  | W   | Th  | F   | Sa  | Su   |
|--------|-----|-----|-----|-----|-----|-----|------|
| Week 5 | Off | E3  | E4  | Off | E3  | E4  | E5   |
| Week 6 | Off | E4  | E5  | Off | E4  | E5  | E6   |
| Week 7 | Off | E5  | E6  | Off | E5  | E6  | E7   |
| Week 8 | Off | E6  | E7  | Off | E6  | E7  | E8   |

|         | M   | Tu  | W   | Th  | F   | Sa  | Su   |
|---------|-----|-----|-----|-----|-----|-----|------|
| Week 9  | Off | E3  | Off | E7  | Off | E7  | E8   |
| Week 10 | Off | E5  | E6  | Off | E5  | E6  | E7   |
| Week 11 | Off | E6  | E7  | Off | E6  | E7  | E8   |
| Week 12 | Off | E7  | E8  | Off | E8  | E9  | E10  |

# INTERMEDIATE PROGRAM

The intermediate program is designed for cyclists with some prior cycling or endurance sport training experience. The rides will be slightly longer and in the later phases more intense than the rides in the beginner program. Throughout this phase, try to focus on pedaling smoothly, keeping your upper body relaxed, and maintaining a good position on the bike. Keep your eyes up, your elbows slightly bent, and your back as flat as possible. Avoid body movement with your pedal stroke and keep your weight balanced so you sit squarely on your saddle. Good habits started in the endurance phase will carry over into your later phases of training. Perform the workouts in the endurance phase at a fairly low intensity. Even though it might be tempting, avoid riding faster than is prescribed for the workout. Remember, the other phases of training will offer plenty of intensity. During this program, you will build up to rides of two hours and 30 minutes.

|  | M | Tu | W | Th | F | Sa | Su |
|---|---|---|---|---|---|---|---|
| **Week 1** | Off | E2 | E3 | Off | E3 | E4 | E5 |
| **Week 2** | Off | E3 | E4 | Off | E5 | E6 | E7 |
| **Week 3** | Off | E4 | E5 | Off | E6 | E7 | E8 |
| **Week 4** | Off | E6 | E7 | Off | E8 | E9 | E10 |

|  | M | Tu | W | Th | F | Sa | Su |
|---|---|---|---|---|---|---|---|
| **Week 5** | Off | E7 | E8 | Off | E8 | E9 | E10 |
| **Week 6** | Off | E7 | E8 | Off | E9 | E10 | E11 |
| **Week 7** | Off | E8 | E9 | Off | E10 | E11 | E12 |
| **Week 8** | Off | E9 | E10 | Off | E11 | E11 | E12 |

|  | M | Tu | W | Th | F | Sa | Su |
|---|---|---|---|---|---|---|---|
| **Week 9** | Off | E3 | Off | E4 | Off | E10 | E11 |
| **Week 10** | Off | E8 | E9 | Off | E10 | E11 | E12 |
| **Week 11** | Off | E9 | E10 | Off | E11 | E11 | E12 |
| **Week 12** | Off | E10 | E11 | Off | E11 | E12 | E12 |

# ADVANCED PROGRAM

The advanced program is designed for cyclists who have a few years of experience in the sport and are motivated to push themselves hard to gain top-level fitness. The rides will be longer and in the later phases will have more intensity than the rides in the beginner and intermediate programs. Perform the workouts in the endurance phase at a relatively low intensity. The next training phases offer plenty of opportunities for intensity. Although holding back your intensity can be difficult, it is important to focus on building your endurance in this program. As you build up to rides of three hours, concentrate on keeping your RPM in the 90 to 110 range and focus on pedaling smoothly and keeping your upper body relaxed. The good habits you develop in this training phase will carry over to the later phases, and they will make you a more efficient cyclist.

|  | M | Tu | W | Th | F | Sa | Su |
|---|---|---|---|---|---|---|---|
| **Week 1** | Off | E4 | E5 | E6 | E7 | E8 | E9 |
| **Week 2** | Off | E5 | E6 | E7 | E8 | E9 | E10 |
| **Week 3** | Off | E6 | E7 | E8 | E9 | E10 | E11 |
| **Week 4** | Off | E7 | E8 | E9 | E10 | E11 | E12 |

|        | M   | Tu  | W   | Th  | F   | Sa  | Su  |
|--------|-----|-----|-----|-----|-----|-----|-----|
| Week 5 | Off | E6  | E7  | E8  | Off | E8  | E9  |
| Week 6 | Off | E7  | E8  | E9  | E2  | E10 | E11 |
| Week 7 | Off | E8  | E9  | E10 | Off | E11 | E12 |
| Week 8 | Off | E9  | E10 | E11 | E2  | E12 | E12 |

|         | M   | Tu  | W   | Th  | F   | Sa  | Su  |
|---------|-----|-----|-----|-----|-----|-----|-----|
| Week 9  | Off | E4  | Off | E5  | Off | E11 | E12 |
| Week 10 | Off | E8  | E9  | E10 | Off | E12 | E12 |
| Week 11 | Off | E9  | E10 | E11 | Off | E12 | E10 |
| Week 12 | Off | E10 | E11 | E12 | Off | E12 | E12 |

156

# 12

# Increasing Lactate Threshold and Strength

After you have a solid foundation, you will begin riding harder and faster. You should dedicate three to four weeks to training your lactate threshold. As explained in chapter 3, a high lactate threshold is one of the best indicators of fitness in an endurance athlete. You can improve your lactate threshold with training, and improving your lactate threshold will be an integral part of your training program.

To improve your lactate threshold, your intensity level during intervals must remain in zone 3—the point that spells the beginning of high-intensity exercise, or more scientifically, the point at which lactic acid removal fails to keep up with lactic acid production. This occurs at a rating of perceived exertion (RPE) level of 6 to 7 and heart rate of 70 to 79 percent of maximal heart rate (MaxHR) and 90 to 99 percent of lactate threshold heart rate (LTHR). The objective is to postpone the onset of lactic acid accumulation, which conserves energy, builds strength, and delays fatigue when you are cycling. After a few weeks of training, you will be able to produce more power (watts) at your LTHR and level 6-7 RPE for a longer time. Your cycling fitness will improve and you will ride faster for longer.

The length of threshold training workouts varies depending on which of the three preparation programs you choose. If you are a beginning rider, you may have a difficult time keeping up with the intensity demands of the advanced program. Also, take into consideration that the beginning program workouts do not extend beyond one hour, while the intermediate and advanced programs do. So, when deciding which program to follow, consider your time constraints and motivation. But also remember that the more you train, the stronger you will get.

# BEGINNER PROGRAM

The beginner program is designed for cyclists who are new to the sport or cyclists who have on average one hour or less to work out each day. Throughout this phase you will complete strength and lactate threshold workouts that are much more taxing than the training in the endurance phase. Therefore, it is important to stay well fueled and hydrated so that you can maintain your energy levels and do the workouts properly. Drinking a high carbohydrate solution during the workout will help you maintain your energy levels and stay hydrated. The first part of lactate threshold workouts feels pretty easy, but they become progressively more difficult. Your muscles will be sore after your first few strength workouts, but they will adapt over time. You will feel a burning sensation in your leg muscles during and after the lactate threshold workouts; this means you have done the workouts correctly. Make sure that you do not ride too hard on your endurance days, or you will not recover properly for the next workouts.

| | M | Tu | W | Th | F | Sa | Su |
|---|---|---|---|---|---|---|---|
| **Week 1** | Off | LT7 | LT1 | Off | LT7 | LT1 | E2 |
| **Week 2** | Off | LT8 | LT2 | Off | LT8 | LT2 | E3 |
| **Week 3** | Off | LT8 | LT3 | Off | LT9 | LT4 | E4 |
| **Week 4** | Off | LT9 | LT4 | Off | LT9 | LT4 | E4 |

# INTERMEDIATE PROGRAM

The intermediate program is designed for cyclists with some prior cycling or endurance sport training experience. The rides in this program are slightly longer and more intense than the rides in the beginner program because this program contains more intervals. The workouts in this phase are much more strenuous than the work you completed in the endurance phase. After the first few strength workouts, your muscles are likely to be sore. Don't worry, though, they will adapt as you continue through the training program. You'll know you're completing the lactate threshold workouts correctly if you feel a burning sensation in your leg muscles during and after each workout. Remember to stay well fueled and hydrated during the workouts so that you can do the workouts properly. Drinking a carbohydrate solution between each interval will help you maintain the energy levels you need. Remember to stay in zone 2 during your endurance rides. If you ride too hard on the endurance days, you will not recover properly for the next interval workout.

| | M | Tu | W | Th | F | Sa | Su |
|---|---|---|---|---|---|---|---|
| Week 1 | Off | LT7 | LT1 | E1 | LT8 | LT2 | E3 |
| Week 2 | Off | LT8 | LT4 | E1 | LT9 | LT3 | E4 |
| Week 3 | Off | LT9 | LT4 | E1 | LT10 | LT5 | E5 |
| Week 4 | Off | LT10 | LT6 | E1 | LT12 | LT11 | E6 |

# ADVANCED PROGRAM

The advanced program is designed for cyclists who have a few years of experience in the sport and are motivated to push themselves hard to gain top-level fitness. The rides are longer and are more intense than the beginner and intermediate programs. The strength and lactate threshold workouts included in this chapter are more demanding than the workouts in the endurance phase. To complete these workouts properly, you must be well fueled and hydrated. You can maintain your energy levels by drinking carbohydrate solutions between intervals. Your muscles will be sore after your first few strength workouts, but they will adapt over time. During and after the workouts you will feel a burning sensation in your leg muscles, but this means you are working hard. To ensure that you're ready for each lactate threshold (LT) workout, complete your endurance rides in the proper zone. If you ride too intensely, it will be difficult to recover for your next LT workout.

|  | M | Tu | W | Th | F | Sa | Su |
|---|---|---|---|---|---|---|---|
| Week 1 | Off | LT8 | LT2 | E1 | LT9 | LT2 | E9 |
| Week 2 | Off | LT9 | LT3 | E1 | LT10 | LT4 | E10 |
| Week 3 | Off | LT10 | LT5 | E1 | LT11 | LT6 | E11 |
| Week 4 | Off | LT11 | LT5 | E1 | LT12 | LT12 | E12 |

## ACTIVE RECOVERY WEEK

After completing your lactate threshold–building phase, you should feel tired. Because you accomplished a lot of work, take five days of active recovery. Don't worry about losing fitness. Your body needs the recovery time to rebuild after all the work during this phase. The recovery week for each program helps prepare your body for the next phase of training, and it is during the recovery week that your body becomes stronger. After five recovery days you will complete a hill test and time trial test to gauge your fitness gains. Remember to keep track of your results in your training diary because you will do these same tests at the end of the next phase. Comparing your results and tracking your improvement will increase your confidence and motivation.

| | M | Tu | W | Th | F | Sa | Su |
|---|---|---|---|---|---|---|---|
| **Beginner recovery week** | Off | E2 | Off | H3 | Off | TT11 | H1 |
| **Intermediate recovery week** | Off | E2 | Off | H4 | Off | TT11 | H1 |
| **Advanced recovery week** | Off | E4 | Off | E6 | Off | TT12 | H1 |

# CHAPTER 13

# Building Toward a Peak

In this three-week phase you will begin to build high-end speed and move further toward your fitness peak. This phase builds all-around cycling fitness through endurance, time trial, and hill workouts. You will train in all five intensity zones in this phase but will do the majority of your intervals in zone 4. Because of the intensity of the training, be sure to fully recover on your rest days so that you can get the most out of each workout. You should come out of this phase at about 85 percent of your peak fitness.

If you are training for a time trial or hill-climbing event, your training should match the type of effort required by your goal event. Substitute time trial or hill-training workouts on high-intensity days.

As in previous chapters, the beginner program here is less vigorous and requires less time than the intermediate and advanced programs. Because this phase pushes your training up a notch from the last phase and the potential exists to burn out or overtrain, choose the same program level that you used for the lactate threshold phase or step down a level if needed. Don't be tempted to step up a level. At the end of this three-week phase, you will be fatigued and will need another active recovery week before moving on to the next phase. The active recovery week is built into each program.

# BEGINNER PROGRAM

The beginner program is designed for cyclists who are new to the sport or cyclists who have on average one hour or less to work out each day. This phase is difficult but will make you strong. Because you will train at an intense level during this phase, make sure that you take it super easy on your days off. This will allow you to recover more easily and to gain more from each workout. Be sure you don't ride too hard during your Sunday endurance ride. Otherwise, you will have a difficult time recovering for your next interval session.

| | M | Tu | W | Th | F | Sa | Su |
|---|---|---|---|---|---|---|---|
| **Week 1** | Off | H2 | TT1 | Off | H3 | TT2 | E4 |
| **Week 2** | Off | H4 | TT4 | Off | H5 | TT6 | E5 |
| **Week 3** | Off | H8 | TT9 | Off | H10 | H9 | E6 |
| **Recovery week** | Off | E3 | OFF | E4 | Off | TT11 | H1 |

# INTERMEDIATE PROGRAM

The intermediate program is designed for cyclists with some prior cycling or endurance sport training experience. The rides are slightly longer and more intense than the rides in the beginner program. The workouts in this phase are mentally and physically tough and require a high level of concentration. Motivate yourself before each interval and be sure to recover fully between them. You will feel fatigued by the end of these three weeks of hill and time trial training, but you will gain an immense amount of fitness during this phase. You will see the improved fitness during your tests in the final week.

|  | M | Tu | W | Th | F | Sa | Su |
|---|---|---|---|---|---|---|---|
| **Week 1** | Off | H2 | TT1 | E1 | H3 | TT2 | E6 |
| **Week 2** | Off | H4 | TT4 | Off | H5 | TT6 | E8 |
| **Week 3** | Off | H8 | TT8 | E1 | H10 | TT9 | E10 |
| **Recovery week** | Off | E4 | OFF | E6 | Off | TT11 | H1 |

## ADVANCED PROGRAM

The advanced program is designed for the cyclists who have a few years of experience in the sport and are motivated to push themselves hard to gain top-level fitness. The rides are longer and are more intense than the beginner and intermediate programs. This phase of your training is extremely challenging. These workouts are mentally and physically tough, and you will need to concentrate to complete this program. Focus on pedaling smoothly and powerfully during each ride. Motivate yourself before the intervals and allow yourself to fully recover between them. Your fatigue level will be high by the end of three weeks of hill and time trial training. The final rest week is critical for you to recover and gain your strength before moving onto the next phase. You will greatly improve your fitness, which you'll see from the results of your tests in the final week.

| | M | Tu | W | Th | F | Sa | Su |
|---|---|---|---|---|---|---|---|
| **Week 1** | Off | H2 | TT2 | E1 | H3 | TT3 | E8 |
| **Week 2** | E1 | H4 | TT4 | E1 | H6 | TT5 | E10 |
| **Week 3** | E1 | H8 | TT7 | E1 | H11 | TT9 | E12 |
| **Recovery week** | Off | E8 | OFF | E8 | Off | TT12 | H1 |

# CHAPTER 14

# Maintaining Peak Condition

During this phase, you will attain peak fitness and maintain it. The length of the phase depends on your goals. A three-week phase allows you to peak for one event. If you want to maintain your peak for a series of events over several weeks, you can train in this phase for up to six weeks. Training takes place in all intensity zones and focuses on speed-work. In comparison to the earlier three phases, this phase includes more recovery days between the high-intensity workouts to allow full recovery. This approach allows you to do high-quality work and keep your legs and mind fresh and in peak condition.

When athletes reach peak condition, they must continue to stimulate the body with intense workouts to maintain the fitness level. But they must also rest more. It takes a few years of riding and racing to realize how important the balance between stimulus and rest is to maintaining a high level of fitness. In the beginning of Dede's career, she often fried her legs soon after reaching peak condition by training too hard each day and not resting enough. As she matured, she learned to take it easy between the hard sessions and was able to maintain a peak for four to six weeks. Learning your capacities and paying attention to your energy levels is vital to your success. Keeping a journal will help you get to know your body better and figure out how much stimulus and rest you need in order to maintain peak condition.

As you do the workouts in this phase, visualize yourself racing during the intense intervals. This will help you to increase the pace an extra notch. As with the earlier training phases, the intermediate and advanced programs are more vigorous than the beginner program.

If you want to maintain your peak fitness for up to six weeks, you need to extend this phase by three weeks. We have provided sample program extensions, but you may want to create your own using the template in the appendix (page 183). When creating these weeks, remember that you must continue to stimulate your lungs and legs by doing the sprint training workouts, but you must also rest enough. You can continue in the program by doing four days a week of sprint training workouts, concentrating mainly on the final five to seven workouts. Do one endurance ride per week and on the other two days you can rest or ride easy. Build more rest days into your program if you do not feel fully recovered and fatigue lingers on a day when hard training is scheduled. Pay attention to your fatigue levels. If you do not feel mentally and physically fresh before each sprint training session, take an extra recovery day. At this phase in your program, your body is like a finely tuned engine—very efficient but slightly fragile. Too much training can put you over the edge and cause fatigue, which will decrease your performance level.

# BEGINNER PROGRAM

The beginner program is designed for cyclists who are new to the sport or cyclists who have on average one hour or less to work out each day. This program has more rest built into it than the intermediate and advanced programs. These workouts, if done correctly, create a lot of lactic acid in your legs, which means they will be sore afterward. But this phase includes additional recovery time so that you're ready for the next intense workout. This maximal intensity allows you to gain maximal speed. Motivate yourself for each interval.

| | M | Tu | W | Th | F | Sa | Su |
|---|---|---|---|---|---|---|---|
| **Week 1** | Off | S10 | S8 | Off | S7 | E4 | S11 |
| **Week 2** | Off | S5 | S8 | Off | S2 | E3 | S12 |
| **Week 3** | Off | S6 | E3 | S8 | Off | E3 | Race, event peak, or fitness test |

| | M | Tu | W | Th | F | Sa | Su |
|---|---|---|---|---|---|---|---|
| **Week 4** | Off | S7 | E4 | S10 | Off | S8 | S10 |
| **Week 5** | Off | S8 | E3 | S12 | Off | E2 | S11 |
| **Week 6** | Off | S6 | Off | S10 | Off | E2 | Race, event peak, or fitness test |

# INTERMEDIATE PROGRAM

The intermediate program is designed for cyclists with some prior cycling or endurance sport training experience. These workouts are all-out, maximal-intensity efforts, and the lactic acid created in your muscles will cause soreness after your efforts. But the program also provides additional recovery opportunities. Because you will be working at maximal intensity, you will gain maximal speed. While doing the intervals in this phase, imagine yourself racing because this will help you to maximize your speed.

|  | M | Tu | W | Th | F | Sa | Su |
|---|---|---|---|---|---|---|---|
| **Week 1** | Off | S5 | S8 | E2 | S6 | E8 | S11 |
| **Week 2** | Off | S10 | S2 | Off | S4 | E3 | S12 |
| **Week 3** | Off | S7 | E4 | S8 | Off | E6 | Race, event peak, or fitness test |

|  | M | Tu | W | Th | F | Sa | Su |
|---|---|---|---|---|---|---|---|
| **Week 4** | Off | S4 | S8 | Off | S4 | E8 | S12 |
| **Week 5** | Off | S6 | E4 | S2 | Off | S8 | S11 |
| **Week 6** | Off | S7 | E5 | S12 | Off | E6 | Race, event peak, or fitness test |

# ADVANCED PROGRAM

The advanced program is designed for cyclists who have a few years of experience in the sport and are motivated to push themselves hard to gain top-level fitness. The rides are slightly longer and are more intense than the beginner and intermediate programs. This program includes many all-out workouts as well as the opportunity to recover so that you'll be prepared for the next set. After your high-intensity efforts, expect to be sore because you will create a lot of lactic acid in your legs. However, by working at maximal intensity, you will gain maximal speed. You can get the most from this phase if you visualize yourself in a race during the workouts. Doing so will help you maximize your speed.

| | M | Tu | W | Th | F | Sa | Su |
|---|---|---|---|---|---|---|---|
| **Week 1** | Off | S2 | S1 | E1 | S10 | S3 | S11 |
| **Week 2** | Off | S5 | E12 | E1 | S11 | S8 | S12 |
| **Week 3** | E1 | E8 | S7 | E12 | Off | E8 | Race, event peak, or fitness test |

|  | M | Tu | W | Th | F | Sa | Su |
|---|---|---|---|---|---|---|---|
| **Week 4** | Off | S7 | E8 | S10 | Off | E1 | S12 |
| **Week 5** | Off | S8 | E7 | S11 | Off | E2 | S12 |
| **Week 6** | Off | S9 | E6 | S12 | Off | E1 | Race, event peak, or fitness test |

# CHAPTER 15

# Cross Training in the Off-Season

Cross training by participating in aerobic exercise and strength building is a great way to stay active in the off-season or winter months. At the end of each season, recharge your batteries by taking time off the bike and perhaps even resting altogether for two to four weeks. After a solid break followed by steady activity throughout your off-season, you will benefit next season from increased strength and endurance.

You will benefit both mentally and physically from engaging in a variety of sports during the off-season, so make an effort to have fun. The variety will keep you mentally fresh and motivated. Physically, you will build strength and endurance, and cross training will help you balance your muscular strength by improving your weaknesses. Cycling, like other sports, develops a specific set of muscles and neglects others. As a result, imbalances develop, which can cause overuse injuries. Cross training reduces the chances of overuse injuries.

During cross training, choose sports you enjoy. Many professional cyclists run, cross-country ski, hike, swim, lift weights, and do yoga in the off-season. You will maintain and build fitness if you engage in endurance exercise four days per week for 20 minutes to three hours at a moderate pace (zone 2, 60 to 69 percent of MaxHR). Mountain biking, running, hiking, cross-country skiing, downhill skiing, telemark skiing, snowshoeing, and swimming are excellent endurance exercises that will help you maintain and build your cycling fitness. Weight-training twice a week will help you build strength. To maintain energy levels throughout the year, take at least one day a week of complete rest throughout the off-season.

Michael and Dede grew up in climates that didn't allow them to ride bikes in the winter, so they ice-skated and skied. Michael played pickup hockey in the evening, and Dede speed-skated on the oval. If you live in a similar climate, pick a sport that keeps your body moving and warm and that also gives you a cardiovascular workout. Now that they live in a warmer climate, Dede and Michael use trails for hiking, mountain biking, and cyclocross riding. Dede loves to run on trails as well. During the off-season you don't need to concentrate on your heart rate, watts, or rating of perceived exertion, but you should stay active, try to refresh your mind, and strengthen the muscles that have been somewhat dormant while you were focused solely on the bike.

© Photodisc

Participating in cross training activities, such as running, can maintain fitness, balance muscle strength, and refresh your mind.

# Core-Strength Exercises

Your abdominal and back muscles are called core muscles for good reason: They are the foundation of the body's stabilization and strength. Because much of the power in your pedal stroke comes from using these core muscle groups, developing a strong core is key to your cycling success. In addition, strengthening your core helps prevent injury, back pain, and fatigue while riding. This chapter includes several core exercises. During the off-season (or off-period of your program), try to engage in these exercises at least twice a week. Start with 10 repetitions of each exercise and build up as you become stronger. Continue these exercises during your cycling season to maintain the benefits.

## Crunches

Lie flat on your back. Lift your knees until the legs are bent at 90 degrees at both the hips and the knees. Cross your arms across your chest and attempt to raise your chin straight up toward the ceiling by contracting your abdominal muscles to lift your shoulders off the ground. The key is to try to keep the movement of your chin vertical and perpendicular to the floor.

## Twist Abdominal Crunches

Lie on your back and cross your arms over your chest. Bend the knees and drop both legs toward the ground on the right side. Lift the knees toward the chest, keeping the low back pressed into the ground, and crunch your abdominal muscles. Repeat on the opposite side.

## Side Abdominal Crunches

Lie flat on your back. Bend your knees, keeping your feet flat on the ground. Place both hands behind your head. Twist your right elbow toward your left knee and do crunches by contracting the abdominal muscles. Be careful not to pull up on your neck with your hands. The movement should be made with your abdominal muscles. Repeat on the opposite side.

## Leg Lifts

Lie flat on your back with your legs straight out. Place your hands behind your head. Lift your heels two to three inches (5-7.5 cm) off the ground. Bring your left elbow and right knee toward each other, hold for a second and then do the same with your right elbow and left knee. Repeat in fairly rapid succession until you are fatigued.

## Back Extensions

It is ideal to use a back extension machine, but if you are doing these exercises at home, here is a simple technique to strengthen your back. Lie facedown with your hands stretched as far above your head as possible. Attempt to lift your arms and legs toward the ceiling, creating an arch in your back. Hold for a few seconds, rest, and repeat.

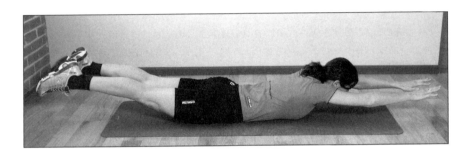

Many stretching and exercise tools are helpful and won't cost you a fortune. If you're willing to purchase a few pieces of key equipment, we recommend a fit ball, foam roller, yoga matt, and a long rubber band. All of these items are inexpensive, and many are portable so you can take them with you when you travel. Although describing exercises using each of these pieces of equipment is beyond the scope of this book, many books are available that can instruct you on equipment usage.

# Weight Training

Weight training will help you balance your musculature and make you a stronger cyclist. The majority of your gym work should consist of circuit training, which entails moving from one weight station to the next with minimal rest between stations. This approach is a great way to work toward both strength and cardiovascular fitness. For example, you would do a set of squats followed by a set of sit-ups and then move directly to the bench press. You should keep your heart pumping and your breathing accelerated to get the most out of your workout. Circuit training not only builds strength, it also works on cardiovascular fitness. In the same way you periodize your cycling workouts, you should cycle your weight workouts. Don't repeat the same workout during the entire off-season. Remember, your body needs change to continue adapting. Numerous books are available on specific weight-training programs. We recommend taking a look at *Fitness Weight Training* by Thomas R.

Baechle and Roger W. Earle for additional guidance. However, the following information will get you started.

If you go to a gym, focus on exercises that strengthen your core and lower body, and don't overdo it with your arms. A little upper-body strength can provide added power when sprinting or climbing during races, but if cycling is your primary athletic activity, you don't want to add too much bulk in your upper body that will weigh you down on the bike. Here is a list of key exercises to build strength in the off-season.

- **Squats.** Use a free-weight squat rack. Stand up straight with your legs shoulder-width apart. Lift the bar onto your shoulders and allow it to rest on your upper back, holding each side with your hands. Squat until the knees are bent 90 degrees. Hold for a few seconds and stand again. Keep your back straight and look up toward the ceiling throughout the exercise.
- **Hip sleds.** Use a hip-sled machine at the gym. Be sure to bend the knees to 90 degrees.
- **Lunges.** Step forward on one foot. Bend the front knee to 90 degrees, keeping the back leg extended behind you. Return to the starting position by pushing off with your front foot. Repeat on the other side. This exercise can be done holding dumbbells or by grasping a free-weight bar with both hands and resting it on the shoulders.
- **Leg extensions.** Use a leg-extension machine at the gym. Be careful not to overextend your knees.
- **Leg curls.** Use a leg curl machine at the gym.
- **Calf raises.** Use a calf machine at the gym.
- **Seated row.** Use a seated-row machine in the gym.
- **Bench press.** Use a free-weight bench in the gym. While lying on the bench, lift the bar off the supports and slowly lower it until it is about two to three inches (5-7.5 cm) above your chest. Lift it by straightening the arms.

# Strength Training Phases

To gain maximal benefit, divide your off-season strength training into phases (see table 15.1). The first phase is a transitional phase, in which your muscles and ligaments adapt to the motions and stress of weight lifting. In the next two phases, building and strength, increase the amount of weight you lift and reduce the repetitions to gain maximal strength. The final phase is the maintenance phase where you maintain your strength while increasing your time cycling. You can continue this maintenance phase throughout your cycling season if desired.

To be effective, weight training should occur at least twice a week during the transitional, building, and strength phases and at least once a week during the maintenance phase. During the transitional phase, you lift very light weight at high repetitions. By initially focusing on low weight and high repetitions, you allow your muscles and tendons to adapt to weight lifting. This prepares you for the more intense training in the strength phase. During the strength phase, you decrease the number of repetitions and increase the weight you push. This builds your muscle mass and strength. During the maintenance phase, you once again increase the repetitions and lower the weight. This preserves the gains made during the building phase and allows a shift to more training time on the bike.

Warm up for 10 minutes on an exercise bike before lifting and stretch before and after each workout. During the transitional and maintenance phases, quickly move from station to station in your circuit. During the strength phase, take a break between each exercise to allow muscle recovery before each set of repetitions. The maintenance phase includes only squats, sit-ups, and back extensions with very light weight (50 to 60 percent of maximum). If you are not experienced with weightlifting exercises, make an appointment with a personal weight trainer at your local gym. Ask the trainer to show you how to properly perform the exercises. This will help you achieve your goals without injury.

## Table 15.1 Strength Training Plan

| Transitional phase | Building phase | Strength phase | Maintenance phase |
|---|---|---|---|
| 2-4 weeks | 3-6 weeks | 3-4 weeks | All season |
| Increase weight each week | Increase weight each week | Increase weight each week | Dynamic effort during work-out (no pause between exercises) |
| 2-5 sets | 4 sets | 5 sets | 3-5 sets |
| 30 repetitions of each exercise | 20 repetitions of each exercise | 8-12 repetitions of each exercise | 30 repetitions of each exercise |

As you put more energy into cycling during the maintenance phase, exclude the leg extensions, seated rows, and bench presses. Only a light weight-training workout is required to maintain strength.

# Alternative Strength-Building Activities

Taking part in a variety of sports throughout the off-season months will keep you mentally fresh and also help to balance your muscular strength. We attribute much of our ability to come into the racing season fit and fresh to our efforts to vary our training throughout the winter. Here are a few alternative activities for building strength and endurance that focus on the core and lower body and are also a lot of fun:

- **Hiking or running uphill.** This is a great way to build leg strength without gaining muscular bulk. Usually, your body weight is sufficient to give you a good workout, but some professionals like to increase the workload by carrying extra weight in a backpack.

- **Telemark skiing.** The motion of telemarking is similar to performing lunges in the gym. This can be a great way to build power and aerobic fitness outside with your friends.

- **Snowboarding and downhill skiing.** Both of these sports mimic squatting in the weight room. Going off to the ski slopes is certainly more entertaining and motivating than going to the gym.

- **Yoga.** Another supplemental off-season workout that will aid your flexibility and help reduce the risk of injury during the season is yoga. Yoga helps loosen your muscles. The flexibility you gain through yoga workouts allows you to maximize your muscle usage during cycling and other activities. The breathing techniques used in yoga can help you learn to control your breath and focus on the rhythm of breathing while cycling.

## SAMPLE CROSS TRAINING PROGRAM

The sample cross training program contains a combination of weight training, hiking, mountain biking, cross-country skiing, swimming, running, snowshoeing, road riding, and telemark skiing workouts. The program provides five days of training and two recovery days per week. Each week also contains two weight training sessions to help you build strength. The program gives you a wide variety of exercises to help you stay mentally fresh and to develop many different muscles in your body, creating balanced strength. The workouts vary in length from 30 minutes to three hours. If you are an advanced cyclist, 30 minutes may not seem like much of a workout. Add time to the workouts as needed. On the other hand, three hours is probably too much if you are a beginning cyclist, so you should shorten the workouts as needed.

|  | M | Tu | W | Th | F | Sa | Su |
|---|---|---|---|---|---|---|---|
| **Week 1** | Off | Circuit weight training | 1 hour hiking | 1 1/2 hours mountain biking | Off | Circuit weight training | 1 hour cross-country skiing |
| **Week 2** | Off | Circuit weight training | 45 minutes swimming laps | 1 hour running | Off | Circuit weight training | 2 hours mountain biking |
| **Week 3** | Off | Circuit weight training | 1 1/2 hours cross-country skiing | 1 1/2 hours snowshoeing | Off | Circuit weight training | 2 1/2 hours mountain biking |
| **Week 4** | Off | Circuit weight training | 2 hours riding on road | 1 hour cross-country skiing | Off | Telemark skiing | 3 hours mountain biking |

The more time and energy you have to cross-train, the more you will gain. If you're short on time, do as much of a workout as you can, and if you have time and energy for more, challenge yourself to do more. If you do not have access to the locations or equipment needed to participate in some of these sports or if you do not enjoy some of them, replace the workouts with one of the other sports listed in this chapter.

# **A**ppendix

## Sample Four-Week Program

| | M | Tu | W | Th | F | Sa | Su |
|---|---|---|---|---|---|---|---|
| **Week 1** | | | | | | | |
| **Week 2** | | | | | | | |
| **Week 3** | | | | | | | |
| **Week 4** | | | | | | | |

From *Fitness Cycling* by Dede Demet Barry, Michael Barry, and Shannon Sovndal, 2006, Champaign, IL: Human Kinetics.

# Index

*Note:* The italicized *f* and *t* following page numbers refer to figures and tables, respectively.

# About the Authors

**Dede Demet Barry** was a professional racer and member of the United States Cycling Team from 1988 to 2004. A 2004 Olympic silver medalist, Barry also won three World Championship medals, two Pan American Games gold medals, two World Cup championships, and six national titles before retiring at the end of the 2004 season. She also was named the 2004 North American Cyclist of the Year.

Barry now writes columns for various cycling and sporting publications, including *VeloNews*; lectures extensively on the topics of training and her experiences as a female athlete; and serves as a coach and consultant with Thrive Health and Fitness Medicine. In her spare time, she enjoys trail running, cross-country skiing, reading, and cooking. She resides in Boulder, Colorado, and Girona, Spain, with her husband, Michael, and son, Liam.

**Michael Barry** has been a professional cyclist since 1998 and a member of Lance Armstrong's cycling team since 2002. The two-time Olympian (1996 and 2004) is also author of the book *Inside the Postal Bus* (2005 VeloPress), which recounts his experiences on Armstrong's U.S. Postal team. Barry has several victories in international races and has placed prominently in the World Championships and World Cup races. In 2003 he was named Canadian Cyclist of the Year by the Canadian Cycling Association.

Barry also writes articles for numerous newspapers, magazines, and Web sites, including the *Toronto Star*, *Pedal* magazine, *VeloNews*, www.thepaceline.com, and www.bike.com. Along with cycling, in his leisure time Barry enjoys mountain biking, hiking, and running. He, his wife, Dede, and their son, Liam, reside in Boulder, Colorado, and Girona, Spain.

**Dr. Shannon Sovndal** is the owner and founder of Thrive Health and Fitness Medicine (Thrive HFM), an elite team of medical doctors, exercise physiologists, and athletes that provides clients with the highest level of personalized health care, life management, and fitness training. Additionally, he serves as a board-certified emergency medicine physician at Boulder Community Hospital in Colorado, the medical director for AirLife Denver, and a physician at the General Center for Clinical Research at the University of Colorado.

Before becoming a physician, Dr. Sovndal raced road bikes in the United States, during which time he won the California/Nevada District Championship as well as many other road races and criteriums. He has written numerous sports-related articles and has lectured to a wide range of audiences on exercise-related topics. Dr. Sovndal is a member of the American College of Sports Medicine and the American College of Emergency Medicine. He attended medical school at Columbia University in New York and completed his residency at Stanford University in California. Dr. Sovndal resides in Boulder, Colorado, with his wife, Jane, and their two sons, Soren and Theron.

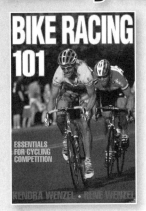
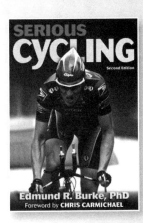
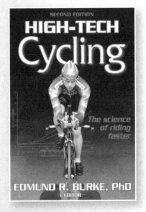
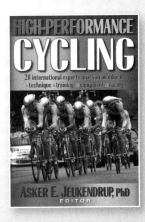